BEGINNER'S GUIDE TO STAMP COLLECTING

Kenneth

This is not philately but guide to one of the world's most popular hobbies—a personal impression of the many pleasures of stamp collecting written by an enthusiast who has been collecting stamps since boyhood.

In addition to dispensing much helpful advice to those taking up stamp collecting for the first time, the author reviews the financial side of the hobby—for stamps can be a sound investment as well as an absorbing pastime—and traces the path ahead from the haphazard accumulation of stamps to the more complex interest of advanced philately. He also places stamps in their context as part of the wider subject of postal history, and deals with the sometimes exaggerated problem of forgeries.

Other chapters refer to such matters as the many different kinds of stamps that can be collected, the lure of postmarks and the appeal of collecting to a theme. All these topics and more are included in a concise survey of a hobby which claims millions of devotees all over the world.

Beginner's Guide to Stamp Collecting

KENNETH W. ANTHONY

SPHERE BOOKS LIMITED
30/32 Gray's Inn Road, London, WC1X 8JL

First published in Great Britain in 1971
by Pelham Books Ltd
© Kenneth W. Anthony, 1971
First Sphere Books edition 1973

TRADE
MARK

Set in Monotype Baskerville

Printed in Great Britain by
Hazell Watson & Viney Ltd,
Aylesbury, Bucks

CONTENTS

ILLUSTRATIONS

ACKNOWLEDGEMENT

Plate Nos. 1–6 inclusive are reproduced by courtesy of Stanley Gibbons Ltd. Plates 8, 11, 12 and 13 are from photographs by Donald S. Herbert.

PREFACE

The purpose of this book is to open up the world of stamps to those who have been attracted to these fascinating bits of gummed paper, but who haven't yet realised the range of interest and satisfaction to be obtained from collecting them.

Assuming virtually no previous knowledge, the book sets out to indicate what the hobby is all about and to answer many of the questions which a beginner is most likely to ask. It is not meant to be a detailed text-book of philately, which would in any case be hardly possible within the bounds of a single volume; it is more of a personal impression of the hobby, an attempt to explain at least some of the reasons why stamps exert such a strong appeal for so many people, and in so doing to offer the beginner a few hints on how to get more enjoyment from his collection.

KENNETH W. ANTHONY

CHAPTER ONE

STAMP APPEAL

Why do people collect stamps? Obviously there must be *something* about these small pieces of coloured paper; otherwise millions of people the world over would not collect them with so much interest and enthusiasm. The answer is easier to experience than to define, and it has been said that there are as many reasons for collecting stamps as there are collectors!

In some ways a liking for stamps is rather like a sense of history or an ear for music; you either have it or you don't have it. Clearly you yourself do have it, for without it you would never have opened this book. And the way to confirm this, of course, is to try the hobby for yourself.

But if I am pressed for an answer to the question, I reply that to me the never-ending appeal of stamps is that they bring the whole world within the covers of an album. At first, stamps were intended merely as convenient receipts for pre-paid postage. But Sir Rowland Hill, the great postal pioneer whose reforms brought about the introduction of the world's first adhesive postage stamps in 1840, started more than he realised.

Even in his day stamps became symbols of the British progress and inventiveness which in the Victorian age led the world. They were also regarded to some extent as paper coins. Immediately we begin to see how stamps began to acquire more than just a postal significance.

Over the past 130 years stamps have become a microcosm of world events. Wars and revolutions, political, economic and social changes – all these are reflected in the stamp album. Stamps indicate national pride and aspirations, disappointments and disasters; they show changes of currency (Britain has provided a recent example!) and inflation; they advertise not only the 'image' of a country but also its products, its industries, even its tourist attractions!

The development of stamp design is itself a subject on which whole books could be written. There are still many collectors of the old school who will tell you that the Penny Black of 1840 was the most beautiful stamp ever issued, but there is no denying that numerous more modern stamps are miniature works of art in their own right.

Take a random assortment of stamps in use in the 1860s and compare them with those of the 1960s. This alone could provide the basis for an interesting collection! The contrast would not be in design alone; there are changes in printing methods to consider, as well as changes in postal rates.

All this explains part of the appeal of stamps. Then there is the 'scientific' aspect. Many collectors like to study the minutiae of stamps (the minor differences of printing and production) and find in this an absorbing relaxation. Stress is said to be the endemic disease of modern times, and it is perhaps significant that many doctors are among the keenest of stamp collectors, discovering in their stamps the ideal leisure retreat from the cares and worries of everyday life.

And as a painless method of acquiring a basic knowledge of world history and geography, stamp collecting is unrivalled! Take a group of your friends and relations (if you dare!) and give the names of St Lucia, St Helena, St Vincent and St Kitts and ask them which one is NOT in the West Indies. Whoever gives you the right answer immediately is probably a stamp collector.

Basically, I suppose, the attraction of stamps can be traced to that acquisitive streak in human nature which finds legal and satisfying expression in the collecting instinct. This has

12

been recognised since ancient times. And stamps have grown in popularity, I believe, because they are so much simpler to collect than so many other things.

Stamps take up very little space. They are clean. They require neither workshop nor elaborate equipment. Above all, stamps are such a flexible pastime. The hobby can be pursued almost anywhere. It is enjoyed by people of all ages and in all walks of life. Owing to their small size and light weight, stamps are easily transported, much more easily, for example, than antique furniture, china or glass! They also require much less protection.

There is another big advantage, too. On stamps one can spend as much or as little time and money as one can afford. While a few stamps are exceedingly rare and sell for hundreds and even thousands of pounds, the great majority of stamps are still reasonably cheap and it is possible to form an interesting and comprehensive collection without great financial outlay.

The youngster taking up the hobby for the first time can add something to his collection every week at the cost of a few new pennies, and get just as much pleasure from his purchases as the learned specialist – perhaps more! Stamp collecting is thus a continuing interest, which does not require long intervals of saving up before each new acquisition.

At the other end of the scale a wealthy man who buys wisely and exercises care and patience can acquire an outstanding collection – perhaps *the* outstanding collection – of a particular country or group of issues for the expenditure of a few tens of thousands of pounds. This sort of outlay, while hopelessly beyond the ambitions of most of us, would go nowhere if the opulent connoisseur started to collect paintings by famous artists, or old silver, or Chippendale furniture, or many other works of art.

The appeal of stamps is universal, and it is the international character of the hobby which helps good stamps to retain and increase their value at a time of depreciating currencies.

This brings me to an advantage which I have deliberately left until last – an advantage which many would say was the most attractive that philately has to offer: the fact that stamps, in addition to being a pleasant and interesting pastime, can also be a good investment! So they can – sometimes. Complete volumes have been published on stamp investment and even in a beginner's guide like this the topic is important enough to deserve a chapter to itself, which it receives later on.

Quite apart from buying stamps for the deliberate purpose of investment, the hobby has another sort of financial appeal: the chance of making a lucky find. To discover some cache of valuable old stamps or covers hidden away in an attic or an old bureau is the dream of every collector – but the experience of very few. It's an unlikely contingency, but if ever it should happen to you, don't tamper with the stamps before obtaining expert advice. In particular, don't remove any stamps from envelopes, and don't separate any blocks of stamps joined together. Otherwise you may destroy a considerable part of their value.

By taking up stamp collecting you are joining the ranks of a hobby which has stood the test of time. In fact stamp collecting is almost as old as stamps themselves. As early as 1842 (when Britain was still the only country in the world issuing stamps) the practice must have been fairly widespread, for in that year *Punch* published a poem making fun of stamp collectors! About this time a lady advertised for large quantities of used postage stamps. The authorities were alarmed, fearing a plot to defraud the Post Office. It turned out that she wanted the stamps to paper the wall of a room!

It didn't take long for other countries to realise that postage stamps were a good idea. Before the 1840s were out their use had spread to a number of European nations, including France, Belgium, Bavaria and the cantonal administrations of Switzerland, as well as to the United States and Brazil. By 1860 only the more remote and backward nations didn't have their own stamps.

The popularity of stamp collecting grew with the number of stamp-issuing countries. Soon collectors began to exchange and trade stamps among themselves. About 1852 a Belgian bookseller, Jean Baptiste Moens, became the world's first stamp dealer. And only four years after that, a young man of sixteen started selling stamps to collectors in a corner of his father's pharmacy in Plymouth. His name was Edward Stanley Gibbons, and he went on to establish perhaps the most famous firm of stamp dealers and philatelic publishers.

In those earnest Victorian times there were a few far-sighted teachers and parents who readily appreciated the educational advantages of stamp-collecting, but they were outnumbered by those who were ready to pour scorn on the hobby, describing it as a pastime fit only for schoolboys, housewives and absent-minded old gentlemen with nothing better to do.

There was, however, nothing like royal patronage to disarm criticism. And the development of the modern appeal of stamp collecting may perhaps be traced back to that day in 1890 when the Duke of Edinburgh, uncle of King George V, opened a stamp exhibition in London and mentioned that his young nephew was a keen collector. In the face of such eminent support and approval, stamp-collecting acquired respectability at last! In 1893 Prince George became an honorary vice-president of the Philatelic Society of London (later to become the Royal Philatelic Society) and later that year the Society gave him a collection of stamps as a wedding present!

Thus stamp collecting well and truly 'arrived' as a reputable hobby, and since then it has never stopped gaining new adherents. Between 1939 and 1945 thousands of

15

people discovered stamps as an ideal means of restful relaxation from the strain of wartime conditions, and since the war the growth of the hobby has been phenomenal.

There is certainly no shortage of stamps to collect; indeed, many people would say there are too many! And the output of new issues from the world's post offices has more than kept pace with the growing number of collectors.

Our grandfathers usually collected the stamps of the whole world, and their target was 'completion': to obtain one example of every stamp ever issued. It was a formidable aim even then, but they were encouraged in their task by the albums of the time: bulky, fixed-leaf affairs which often had a list of stamps printed on the left-hand page, and printed spaces for the same stamps neatly arranged on the opposite page.

One still comes across these old albums occasionally, even today, and to turn their leaves is to see philately as it used to be. The trouble with such albums, of course, was that they allowed no scope whatever for individuality in the scope of the collection or in its presentation. They also quickly became out-of-date, even though many of them left a few blank pages at the back of the volume for new issues. But they served their purpose well enough for the simple-life collector who wanted 'one of each' and no more, and didn't want the trouble of writing-up his collection.

Nowadays, however, there are so many stamps in existence that whole-world collecting of the sort practised half a century ago is virtually impossible, even if time and money were unlimited. It follows that the modern collector, if he is to impose some form and limit on his collection, must restrict his interests to certain fairly well-defined areas of the stamp world. He may collect stamps of the British Commonwealth only – in itself a huge prospect – or just the Scandinavian countries, or the West Indies, or the Pacific Islands, or any other country or group of issues which takes his fancy.

This is called selective collecting, and it is not to be confused, in the philatelic sense, with specializing, which implies an advanced collection and advanced knowledge to go with it. One sometimes hears a young collector say that he specializes, for example, in Canada, when what he means is that he collects only or mainly the stamps of Canada.

There are still many collectors of long experience about, whose interests are so wide that they can be called general collectors, and philately would be the poorer without them. But their collections are often selective from the chronological instead of the geographical point of view: being restricted, perhaps, to stamps issued up to the year 1930, or 1945. This is a method which has much to commend it. If your interests lie in a particular period of history in a particular part of the world, why not collect the stamps in use at that time?

It is interesting to find, however, that many collectors who may be great experts in one particular field often like to broaden their horizon by forming straightforward collections of something quite different: perhaps even a 'magpie' collection in which they keep any odds and ends that happen to appeal to them.

Although this book is intended to help newcomers to the hobby to obtain more pleasure from stamps, it must always be remembered that stamp collecting is a personal hobby, in which no two collections are ever quite identical, in which the golden rule is that there are no rules, in which everyone is free to please himself. That, too, is an important part of stamp appeal!

CHAPTER TWO

MAKING A START

To those about to take up stamp-collecting for the first time,
or to revive a boyhood interest, my advice would be: Do
not rush into it. Take your time. Study other people's
collections, as many different kinds as you can. Gaze at the
stamps on display in stamp dealers' windows. Read everything you can find about stamps. And meanwhile keep all
the stamps that come your way.

If you have no childhood collection on which to build, one
of the best ways of obtaining a general world-wide view of
philately is to buy a big, whole-world packet of stamps from
a dealer. When you have sorted them out into countries,
have studied their designs and inscriptions and learned
something about them, then you have completed your first
philatelic lesson! Before long, almost inevitably, your interest
will be drawn to some particular phase of the hobby, and
this can happen in any one of a great number of ways.

One of the most famous stamp collectors was President
Franklin Roosevelt. Stamps were his lifelong interest, and
were a consolation when, as a young man, he was stricken
with polio. Even in the darkest days of the Second World
War this American statesman found comfort in his stamps.
'I could almost say,' he wrote, 'that I owe my life to my
hobbies – especially stamp collecting.' It was a highly
personal collection, many of the items recalling some
particular occasion in his life. But the only part of it that
was of a specialized nature consisted of the stamps of Hong
Kong, and that was because in his young days the future
president had an aunt living in Hong Kong and his interest
was aroused by the stamps on her letters.

Frequently it is just this kind of fortuitous circumstance that determines the scope of a collection. You may have friends or relations in some distant part of the world; you may have business interests in an overseas country; or you may have spent a holiday abroad and admired the stamps you used on the postcards you sent to friends and neighbours in England.

Such interest will be even stronger if you have lived for any length of time in an overseas country for this will give you some invaluable local knowledge which may well be useful in adding to the interest and worth of your collection.

But it is wise to have regard to other considerations, as well as purely personal ones, before deciding what to collect. To start off with too wide a field could prove discouraging.

To collect the whole of Europe, for example, would prove a daunting task, considering that many of the leading European nations have issued well over a thousand stamps apiece. But you could collect stamps up to a certain limit of face value only, or you could collect the stamps only of one particular period. You could omit or include stamps issued to commemorate special events as distinct from those meant for everyday use for postage.

Or you could break away altogether from geographical considerations and collect stamps not according to the country of issue, but by the subject of the design which is a relatively new development of the hobby which will be considered in a later chapter.

There is also the question of availability. How easy is it going to be to get the stamps you have in mind? The stamps of the major nations of the world, with large populations, are not as a rule going to present a problem. On the other hand there is no denying the exotic and primitive appeal of the stamps from some remote place such as Mongolia or Albania or one of the smaller Indian native states. But such material as exists is going to take a lot of finding, and is not likely to be cheap when it does come on the market. The collector will have to do much searching and exercise plenty of patience, and even then his progress is likely to be slow. Against this, however, when one has once acquired a certain knowledge of the issues of one of these out-of-the-way places, there is always the splendid chance of picking up a bargain from some less knowledgeable individual who doesn't realise its worth. That is part of the fun of stamp-collecting!

You are much less likely to find a scarce item going for a song among the stamps of some more widely collected country like Britain, France or the United States.

At the other extreme it is possible to choose an unmanageably wide field. China, for example, would offer many off-putting difficulties for the beginner, not the least of which would be the problem of learning to recognise at least some of the oriental script seen on Chinese stamps. The various political changes, the varying value of the currency in different parts of this vast land, the sundry occupation issues – to say nothing of the European post-offices in China which formerly issued their own stamps – are an absorbing study which some specialists have made almost their life's work; but the sheer quantity and complexity of the material would make it unsuitable for the newcomer.

An obvious choice of collectors in Britain is, of course, to collect the stamps on their own doorstep – British ones. They may lack the 'foreign'-ness which is part of the attraction of stamp collecting on a wider front, but they have the advantage of being readily available and of presenting absolutely no language problem! One may also be able to keep the collection up-to-date at least partly from one's personal post each morning.

This is philately with a strictly local appeal. One could do a lot worse than collect stamps used in one's own home town or district.

British stamp designs have often been criticised as un-

exciting and maybe they are, on the surface. But Bɹ
after all, was the home of the world's first adhesive po:
stamps and to many people the early engraved issues fɪ
the Penny Black onwards have a simple dignity and beaᴜ
all their own. Indeed the Penny Black and its companior.
the lesser known but rarer Twopence Blue, set a fashion in
stamp design which despite all modern developments has
persisted in some respects to the present time.

The Queen's head was chosen for the first stamps as being
an extremely difficult design to forge, and also from the
analogy of the coinage, which since Roman times had
always carried the head of the sovereign.

As the prosperity and literacy of Victorian Britain increased, so the need arose for stamps to be printed more
quickly and in ever larger quantities. Thus the early
engraved stamps were replaced, from 1855 onwards, by the
less handsome surface-printed stamps.

British stamps have always been thought of, at least until
the flurry of brightly coloured commemorative issues of the
last few years, as conservative and traditional. Yet Britain
has been a stamp pioneer in many ways. The British Post
Office was not only the first to issue stamps; it was the first
to bring out perforated stamps, so that they could be easily
separated without the aid of scissors. And in more recent
years it has been the first to produce stamps specially
treated for use in electronic sorting equipment: stamps with
black graphite lines on the back, and shiny phosphor lines
on the front.

The style of British stamps, like those of other nations, re-
flects changing times. The proud lion of the British Empire
Exhibition stamps of 1924 and 1925 symbolises a world of
imperial greatness quite out of fashion today – and the
short-lived stamps of King Edward VIII, of which only
four values were issued prior to the abdication, remind the
collector of a crisis unparalleled in the history of the British
monarchy.

, there is plenty of interest in British stamps. But they been studied to an extremely specialized degree, with result that competition for desirable material is keen, ..d prices are accordingly high. Fortunately, however, the ,eneral run of issues was printed in such huge quantities that used examples of the majority of British stamps are well within the reach of the majority of collectors.

A comprehensive collection of British stamps reveals some interesting fluctuations in postage rates. Many were gradually reduced up to the years immediately preceding the First World War, when postage was cheaper than it has been at any time before or since. After that the changes were mainly upwards.

Among British collectors the most popular stamps apart from those of Britain itself are the issues of the British Commonwealth. Many of the early stamps of the most favoured colonies, notably those in the West Indies, are nowadays both rare and expensive. But if you start from the reign of King George VI a collection becomes a more manageable proposition.

British Commonwealth stamps, like so many others, illustrate history in the making. Stamps tell the story as various colonial territories first acquire new constitutions, then internal self-government and finally complete independence, sometimes changing their names in the process. The erstwhile Gold Coast has become Ghana, Nyasaland is now Malawi, the old Northern Rhodesia is the new Zambia, and the former British Guiana has become Guyana. The 1960s have introduced many new names to the stamp album.

Unfortunately some of these 'new' nations have been over-enthusiastic in providing themselves with new issues. They have been so numerous that a good many collectors have decided to call a halt after the post-independence stamps and have turned their attention to older issues.

The number of new stamps, in fact, tends to increase year

by year in most parts of the world. Face value, too, shows a rising trend as postal rates keep pace with depreciating currencies. The result is that collecting new issues is becoming steadily more expensive. To obtain one mint example of every new stamp issued by all the countries of the Commonwealth meant an outlay of about £150 in 1968. In the following year the cost rose to more than £200.

These apparently alarming figures do, however, include every issue of the year right up to the highest face value – and in a growing number of countries that means £1 denominations and higher. To buy the Commonwealth new issues of 1968 up to the 2s. 6d. value or equivalent cost around £100 and the figure for 1969 was about the same.

The answer for the British Commonwealth collector may therefore be in many cases to select a few of his best-liked territories for favoured treatment, keeping these up-to-date with all new issues at modest cost, and then adding some second favourites, collecting these only up to, say, 1960, or some other date that seems significant in the country concerned, or alternatively fixing a relatively low limit of face value.

The Queen Elizabeth II issues of the Commonwealth have been described as the most popular stamps in the world. Have they, I wonder, become almost too popular? One sees so many modern Commonwealth collections with page after page of pictorial colonial stamps which are most attractive in themselves but lose something of their appeal because they are seen so often.

One outcome of the transition from Empire to Commonwealth, however, has been to lend much greater variety to the stamp issues. Within the Commonwealth group you can collect stamps for the tiny island community of Tristan da Cunha or the teeming millions of India; for the great dominions of Canada and Australia or the up-and-coming nations like Jamaica and Malaysia. Nowadays their stamps are all very different from one another, but fifty years ago

23

you could find stamps of the same basic design being used in Ceylon, Sierra Leone, Fiji and Hong Kong!

Then there are the countries which are undeniably part of the Commonwealth group but have always had their distinctive appeal. Two examples which quickly spring to mind are Sarawak, where the remarkable white rajahs used to rule, and the native Pacific kingdom of Tonga.

The philatelic story of Rhodesia would easily fill a book. Its early stamps were issued by the British South Africa Company, one of the old chartered companies which did so much to develop the further-flung outposts of Empire. (Even the famous East India Company survived into the stamp era, and another in the stamp-issuing category is the British North Borneo Company.) Then came the division into Northern and Southern Rhodesia, each with its own stamps; next the issues of the short-lived Central African Federation of Rhodesia and Nyasaland; then the transition of the former Southern Rhodesia into the modern Rhodesia.

English collectors adopted a tolerant air of amusement when the Americans were forbidden to possess stamps of North Korea, Red China and North Viet-Nam, on the grounds that their purchase would assist the enemy economy. Now the boot is on the other foot, and at the time of writing it is illegal for British collectors to obtain any mint stamps of Rhodesia issued since the present Salisbury regime made its unilateral declaration of independence. The ban does not apply to used stamps received on mail sent through the post in the ordinary way, and of course there is no restriction as regards Rhodesian stamps issued up to 1965. But this is the first time in upwards of one hundred and thirty years that the British Government has intervened to instruct collectors on what they should or should not collect.

Almost every Commonwealth country has an interesting story to tell in stamps, and in this large group there is clearly enough and to spare to last most collectors a lifetime. Nevertheless I always feel that a collector is missing something

24

worth while if, when deciding the bounds of his collection, he does not include at least one country from the Foreign sector. (In philately 'Foreign' tends to mean anything outside the British Commonwealth and its related countries such as Eire and South Africa.)

For one thing, with foreign stamps not being so widely collected in this country, you are likely to get better value for your money. A scarce stamp of Bulgaria will cost you a lot less than a British stamp of equal scarcity, though it may well take rather more finding. You will also be less likely to finish up with a collection looking like a duplicate of the next man's.

There are many promising contenders in the foreign sector. German stamps have always had a special appeal to me because they are so varied in character.

One may begin with perhaps a modestly representative lot of the less expensive stamps of the old German States, issued before the country was unified. With the philatelic effects of the Franco-Prussian war one detects the emergence of Prussia as a world power, resulting in the first stamps of the German Empire. Then follow the occupation stamps of the First World War, the republican issues of the 1920's, the impact of the Nazis and the propaganda stamps of the Second World War period. Next one sees the issues of the Allied Military Government and now the stamps of the two Germanies, West and East, and the separate issues for West Berlin. Nothing illuminates modern European history better than a collection of German Stamps!

For sheer artistry of design and engraving the stamps of Austria and France over the past twenty-five years take some beating. The Latin American countries are less popular than they used to be, but there is a happy hunting ground here, too. The compact Scandinavian group has its followers, or if you are looking for something rather more off the beaten track you could try Turkey or Iran.

The United States are interesting because although the

commemorative stamps are very numerous, they are invariably of low face value and obtainable easily and cheaply. America is an example of stamp design being used as a deliberate policy to reflect history, traditions and a way of life, welding together people of many different extractions into a great nation.

In the same way Soviet Russia has been even more prolific in its production of large, multihued stamps to emphasise Russian achievements. In a ten-year period, 1955–65, there were rather more than 1,200 of them (an average of 120 new stamps a year) which most collectors would consider rather too many! In general the face value is considerably higher than the corresponding American stamps, too, so it is not surprising that interest in Russian stamps, at least the commemoratives, is at a low ebb.

Whatever the final selection – and as has been seen, the choice is wide – the aim will then be to secure a reasonable degree of completion within the chosen sector, however limited it may be at first. You can always add new interests later on. In these days *absolute* completion is of course hardly possible. Sooner or later progress on your favourite country will probably come to a halt for a time while the search for some specially elusive stamp goes on. But by that time there is sure to be some other philatelic byway beckoning you. Stamp collecting is a hobby that has no end!

In the great majority of cases, new issues help to keep the interest alive and growing. There is always the prospect of examining new stamps as they appear to discover anything unusual or unexpected about them. A few collectors, on the other hand, plough a solitary but happy furrow entirely in the past.

These are the people who collect 'dead' countries. In philatelic parlance a dead country is one which has either ceased to exist as such or for some reason no longer issues stamps. The pre-World War One countries of Serbia, Montenegro and Bosnia (all now incorporated into Yugo-

26

slavia) are obvious examples. So are the old German and Italian States which lost their independence in the movements towards national unity. A somewhat curious case was Danzig, a German seaport on the Baltic which became a 'free state' (with its own stamps) in the political settlement after the First World War until Hitler took over in 1939. It is now part of Poland.

'Dead' countries in the Commonwealth group include the old Canadian provinces, Australian states, and South African provinces, all of which had their own stamps at one time. Another example is Heligoland. It is not often remembered nowadays that this island off the German coast was once British: issuing its own stamps (some with the head of Queen Victoria) until 1890, when it was handed over to Germany in exchange for certain rights in East Africa. A country which more recently disappeared from the list of stamp-issuing authorities is Newfoundland, which joined the Canadian Confederation in 1949.

A still more recent (and more tragic) example was provided by Biafra, which issued its own stamps for a year or so. A somewhat comparable case occurred across the Atlantic more than a century ago: the stamps of the Confederate States may still be mounted in the album – perhaps to the ghostly strains of 'Dixie'!

Dead countries have their advantages – certainly there is no need to fear missing the latest new issue while you are away on holiday – but to start with, at least, I think the newcomer will be better advised to stick to live ones.

Nevertheless it can add greatly to the interest of the collection to delve back into the forerunners of your chosen country. A collector of South African stamps, for instance, will probably like to have at least a few examples in his album of the Cape of Good Hope, Natal, Transvaal and Orange Free State. In fact the early issues are necessary to explain the more modern stamps of South Africa, with their inscriptions in both English and Afrikaans to accord with the

27

bilingual nature of the country. This is so even though since 1967 the designers of South African stamps have craftily adopted the abbreviation 'RSA' which stands for 'Republic of South Africa' in both languages!

In contrast to the dead countries, the collector who prefers modern stamps to old ones may like to choose a country which has arrived on the philatelic scene in comparatively recent years. Pakistan, which first issued stamps in 1947, is one of these; Israel, which started in 1948, is another. Stamps for Pitcairn, which always conjure up pictures of the Mutiny on the Bounty, did not begin until 1940. Other things being equal, there is obviously a better chance of forming a fairly complete collection of countries like these than of nations with a longer stamp-issuing history.

On the other hand the rate at which stamps are issued is also important. Pakistan managed to issue about three hundred different stamps in its first twenty-three years; Pitcairn took seven years longer to issue only a third as many.

Australian stamps are extremely popular with collectors; so are New Zealand's. But a beginner will find Australia less formidable since the first stamps for the whole country, replacing those of the Australian states, did not appear until 1913, whereas New Zealand has been issuing stamps since 1855.

Before making up your mind it is worth while bearing in mind such considerations as these and checking up on the stamps so far issued (both in numbers and in value) of the country or countries you have in mind. To do this you will need to refer to a catalogue – and this is the subject of Chapter 4. Having found out, you may prefer something a little less ambitious, leaving your first choice to be followed up in a few years' time!

A question which beginners often ask is: 'Should I collect mint stamps or used stamps?' The only real answer is: 'Whichever you prefer.' Stamps issued up to about thirty years ago are in most cases a good deal cheaper used than unused, so unless you have a deep purse the question may thus solve itself as far as the older issues are concerned. Modern stamps are often more readily obtainable unused. Some people contend that a postage stamp is not really complete until it has fulfilled its primary purpose and has been postally used, with a postmark to show for it. There is much to be said for this point of view. Unused stamps require more careful handling, and an all-mint collection means no interesting postmarks, which seems a pity. On the other hand there can be no denying that a well-arranged page of stamps in brilliant mint condition is a splendid sight to behold, and minor varieties are more easily seen on unused stamps than on used. Most collections contain both used and unused stamps.

After all the discussion about selective collecting, I must confess to a certain sneaking sympathy for the independent-minded collector who turns his back on all such matters and determines to collect just a few stamps from each and every country in the world. Well, that's his privilege!

Certainly there seem no bounds to the ingenuity of collectors in finding new ways of collecting. At an important exhibition I once saw a display consisting entirely of stamps of a farthing face value – and most interesting it was, too.

Having decided at leisure what stamps you would like to collect, how do you set about obtaining them? That question I will endeavour to answer in the next chapter.

CHAPTER THREE

SOURCES OF SUPPLY

Obviously the nicest way of obtaining stamps is to get them for nothing. Junior collectors often start with the gift of an old collection from some relative, or the present of a packet of stamps for birthday or Christmas. Some stamp dealers provide gift vouchers to make present-buying easy, and since collectors interests are so widely different it has always surprised me that the stamp trade haven't taken up vouchers with more enthusiasm.

Some fortunate individuals are in a position at their place of business to obtain stamps free from overseas correspondence. Many a useful stamp has been retrieved from an office waste paper basket! But the really large business houses, such as the banks, have cottoned on to this source of revenue and sell the envelopes from their mail in bulk to dealers.

As already stated, an excellent way to get the 'feel' of stamps is to buy a large mixed packet to study, perhaps while you are still making up your mind as to what form the collection will eventually take. In this way you will, of course, obtain some stamps which won't fit your final plan. Never mind. Put it down to your philatelic education – and in any case you will have the nucleus of an accumulation of duplicates and unwanted stamps which with luck and perseverance you will be able to dispose of to other collectors, and with the proceeds obtain stamps that you do want.

If you are starting in this way, it pays to buy the largest packet you can afford. A whole-world packet of 500 stamps, all different, will cost about 40p. A packet of 1,000 may be priced at about £1. The cost per stamp is certainly a little more in the larger packet, but you will still get ten stamps per new penny. If you buy a small packet first and then progress to a larger one, the latter is likely to duplicate a fair number of the stamps in the first. The large packet does at least guarantee that you will have 1,000 *different* stamps to start your collection.

From this beginning you may well find that some countries are quite well represented, and others not at all. This too may help you to settle the form your collection will take.

If, for example, you decide to develop a collection of Canada, the next stage could be to buy what is known as a one-country packet. A packet of 100 Canadian stamps can be bought for about 40p. If your choice is a less popular country, or one where there are fewer common stamps in plentiful supply, a one-country packet of similar size could be more expensive. Again, a packet containing a high proportion of commemorative and pictorial issues could cost a little more than run-of-the-mill material. As the range is restricted the cost per stamp goes up once more, but is still much less than it would be if the same stamps were bought individually.

An interesting way of obtaining stamps which may give the collector many hours of pleasure is to buy an old general collection and go through it carefully. Dealers have been known to accept low prices for bulky old collections of this kind, just to get them out of the way! They were acquired in the first place, probably, because the dealer noticed in the battered, elderly album a few worth-while stamps for which he had customers waiting or which he wanted to put into stock. The remainder, consisting of fairly common stamps, or perhaps a few quite scarce ones in damaged condition, are of little interest to him.

To the beginner, however, they present a fine opportunity. And since few dealers can spare the time to examine every single stamp carefully, there is always the chance that something good may have been overlooked! Again you will in any case add to your store of duplicates, but by studying a lot more stamps you will also add to your store of knowledge.

You are now ready to consider other sources of supply. Approval selections are one of the most popular. The dealer mounts stamps on a sheet or in a booklet, prices them individually or in sets, and sends them out on approval to collectors who have asked to see them. The advantage of approval buying is that it gives you the chance of examining stamps at leisure, in the comfort of your own home, and with your collection at hand for comparison.

Most approval business is done by post, frequently as the result of a collector replying to an advertisement. Some dealers, appealing mainly to juniors, offer free gifts of stamps to introduce their approvals. There is no obligation to buy any stamps from the approval book accompanying the gift, but it is, I feel, hardly playing the game to accept the free stamps unless you are prepared to spend at least, say, 30p or 40p on the approvals.

In some cases you will find that dealers offer discounts, sometimes quite substantial ones, on purchases over a given amount. This is to encourage you to make a purchase big enough to justify the dealer's time and trouble. To offer a really enticing discount, however, the dealer may well have put up the prices of his stamps compared with his competitors. When better-quality stamps are sent out on approval, it is unusual to find any discount at all.

When you ask a dealer for approvals, it will save both your time and his if you can describe as exactly as possible the sort of stamps you wish to see, and also your top buying price per stamp. In time the dealer will get to know your interests and will put by anything that comes in that he thinks you may like to have.

Every now and again there is something of an outcry about the practice of sending out unsolicited approvals.

Frankly I don't think the usual criticism of inertia selling methods applies in this case. Collectors usually like to look at stamps, even if they don't intend to buy, and if the dealer encloses return postage I cannot see how any reasonable collector can object to receiving approvals, even if they are unsolicited. After all, it takes only a few seconds to put the approval booklet back in its envelope and return it to the sender. If approvals should arrive so frequently as to become a nuisance, all that is required is a brief note to the dealer telling him not to send any more. In any case he is unlikely to keep it up for long if you never buy anything!

If you are buying unused sets of new issues, it is worth remembering that such stamps are usually at their cheapest immediately after they are first released. As soon as they are withdrawn in the country of issue, and stocks begin to get low, then prices will rise. In large countries, such as Australia and Canada, used stamps, or at least those which remain current over a reasonable period of time, tend to get cheaper as time goes on and the stamps are seen in large numbers in the mails. But this is not the case with small places like Tristan da Cunha, where the amount of postal traffic is very limited and used stamps are generally less easily obtained, and therefore more expensive, than unused supplies.

When you have once decided to acquire, as a matter of lasting policy, all the new issues as they appear of a certain number of countries, then the best and cheapest means of getting them, and making sure that you don't miss any, is by subscribing to a new issue service.

Many leading dealers operate a new issue service, undertaking to supply all the new issues of a particular country or countries in regular distributions at a fixed percentage over face value or cost. Because the dealer has an assured market for the stamps, he can provide them at rather less than the usual new-issue prices in his shop. The collector, to keep his part of the bargain, agrees to accept and pay for the stamps sent, until such time as he gives due notice of his wish to withdraw from the service.

New issue services vary both as to the services provided and the terms offered, and it is worth while to obtain details of several before deciding which one will suit your needs best. The scheme is often extremely flexible: many dealers give you the choice of taking your favourite countries up to varying limits of face value, including or excluding commemorative stamps, postage dues and so on. At least one dealer will also supply such ancillary items as stamp booklets and airletter sheets on a new issue service basis.

It is time now to introduce you to one of the most enjoyable means of both obtaining stamps and of disposing of unwanted ones. This is the circulating exchange packet. The term is really a misnomer, for the aim is to buy and sell stamps rather than exchange, and the so-called 'packet' is in fact a substantial box containing booklets in which stamps for sale are mounted and priced.

The packet is assembled by the organiser, who prepares a list of members to whom it is to be circulated. The collector at the top of the list receives it first, examines the contents, and takes out the stamps he wishes to buy. He then sends a form with his remittance to the organiser, passing the packet to the second member on the list. Before the packet eventually finds its way back to the organiser, it may have been seen by thirty or forty different collectors. You can be a buying member, a selling member, or both.

A few people have assured me that they have formed excellent collections for nothing by the process of buying up old mixed lots and collections, taking out the stamps they needed, and then getting all their money back by sending the residue on the rounds of a circulating exchange packet! I am quite sure this can be done by the exercise of knowledge, time and patience – underlining my contention that stamp collecting can be enjoyed without necessarily spending large sums of money.

The person at the top of the circulation list, of course, gets first choice of all the stamps in the packet. To make sure that every member gets this advantage in turn, the next time a packet starts on its rounds the collector who was previously second on the list moves to the top, and the one previously at the top goes to the bottom.

Some exchange packets are run as commercial enterprises by the organiser, who recovers his expenses and makes his profit from a commission charged on sales. Others are run by local stamp clubs and philatelic societies, in which case the society's funds benefit from the modest commission. These latter have the advantage of being arranged usually to circulate within a limited local area so that the packet can be passed round by hand, thus avoiding the cost of registered postage.

Exchange packets of a more advanced nature are also operated with great success by specialist groups catering for the collectors of a particular country or group only – and when you aspire to specialist status it will be worth your while to inquire about these.

By sundry means, sooner or later, you will have completed a reasonable display, probably, at least of the more common stamps of your chosen country, and you will perhaps have added some attractive modern sets and new issues. Then you will realise that your collection is still suffering from annoying gaps: the odd single stamp here and there, for example, that you require to complete particular sets or issues.

Here we come to another admirable philatelic institution: the wants list. And that is exactly what it is, a list of the stamps you want! Some dealers have departments specially organised to deal with wants lists, providing convenient forms for you to fill in with all the details. The wants must be clearly identified, of course, by the numbers they are given in a recognised catalogue or by date of issue, value, etc., also indicating whether used stamps or unused are required.

The usual system is that all the wants in stock when your list arrives are dispatched forthwith, on approval. No dealer, however large and efficient, can claim to have in stock every stamp ever issued; so the rest are recorded and are sent as soon as they come into stock. It is important to keep your list up-to-date. Send the dealer a revised list from time to time, telling him to cancel the old one. Otherwise he may go to some trouble getting a particular stamp for you, and when it arrives you may have the embarrassing task of explaining that you have just bought it from someone else!

Yet another method of obtaining stamps is at auction. Many of the great rarities change hands in this way, and the publicity given to them may perhaps make the beginner feel that the auction room is no place for him. True, the big London auction houses appeal mainly to advanced collectors with plenty of money to spend, and to dealers. But a little lower down the scale are the various highly reputable provincial auction firms, and much of the material in their sales is within the reach of the average collector.

Sometimes some fine single-country lots can be acquired at provincial auctions – especially if your preference is for some of the more out-of-the-way countries. If stamp auctions are ever held in your own home town you will find it both interesting and worthwhile to attend. The lots can be examined before the sale takes place, and this is another opportunity for the newcomer to extend his knowledge both of stamps themselves and of stamp values. If you cannot attend the sale in person you can obtain the catalogue in advance, study the descriptions (which are most carefully and accurately drawn up by experts), and submit bids by post.

There are also the auctions run by local philatelic societies. These are extremely friendly and informal affairs, in which many of the lots are worth perhaps £1 or even less. The competition is naturally much less keen than at the larger provincial auctions, and excellent bargains can often be obtained. For one thing, the sellers may be prepared to let their unwanted stamps go cheaply as a means of helping the society.

No consideration of the means of acquiring stamps would be complete without a word on the importance of condition. With the growth of the hobby, collectors have paid increasing attention and attached increasing value to the condition of stamps. Generally speaking it may be said that the value of an old and scarce stamp in fine condition is many times that of a defective copy, while many modern issues are virtually worthless unless they are in first-class condition.

Ideally, to qualify as collectable every stamp should be clean, undamaged, and unfaded. If perforated, all the perforations should be intact, and it should be 'well-centred', that is to say, the design should appear centrally within the perforations so that the margins are not uneven. If imperforate, the stamp should have clear margins all round the design. If unused, the stamp should be unblemished, with the original gum still adhering to the back, in fact, just as it was issued by the post office. If used, it should be clearly but not too heavily postmarked.

Of course, condition is a relative term. You can hardly expect the average stamp first issued a century or more ago to be in the same pristine state as the latest new issue. Inevitably the majority of these older stamps have suffered some loss of freshness at the hands of generations of collectors.

The same applies to used stamps. Some are much more easily obtained in good condition than others. The later Victorian stamps of Great Britain, for example, suffered at the hands of 'killer' postmarks which in many cases virtually obliterated the design! It follows that such stamps with a light cancellation fetch a considerable premium.

For beginners the best principle is to acquire stamps in

the best possible condition that you can find or afford, without setting your sights impossibly high. Most people would prefer to have a second-rate example of a rare stamp in their collections rather than a gap – and this, I think, is perfectly justifiable until such time as you can obtain a better one. But there is really no excuse for the scruffy, torn or faded examples of quite common stamps that I have seen in some junior albums. They spoil the appearance of the whole collection.

CHAPTER FOUR

USING THE CATALOGUE

When the world's first stamp catalogue was published in Paris, as long ago as 1861, it listed just over 1,000 stamps–not quite all that had been issued up to that time, but the great majority. With its forty-three small pages, this pioneer was a far cry from the fat volumes of today, when it takes well over seven hundred large and well-filled pages to catalogue the issues of the British Commonwealth alone.

Modern collectors are indeed fortunate in the wealth of literature available to aid them in their hobby, and the heart of this literature is certainly the catalogue. Without a catalogue, the collector is collecting in the dark.

First of all, it is worth pausing to consider exactly what a catalogue is. It is certainly the result of many years of research. That is not to say that every catalogue is necessarily infallible! But the standard of accuracy, in their general information if not in their pricing, is remarkably high.

A catalogue is a work of reference which lists stamps in appropriate sequence as completely as possible within its self-imposed limits. It usually illustrates and describes the designs of the stamps which it lists, and it gives the compiler's view of the retail value of each stamp mentioned. Some catalogues are also the price lists of their publishers (Gibbons is an outstanding example) but this is not true of them all. Some are quite independent publications, produced by people who are not dealers, in which case the valuations are just the editor's opinion and nothing more.

To a newcomer the first sight of a catalogue, especially if it happens to be a fairly advanced one, is a daunting experience, but in fact catalogues are easy to use when you have once learned your way around them. For the beginner, studying the catalogue is the best way of learning a good deal about stamps in a short time.

From the catalogue the collector can learn just what there is to collect; what particular stamps look like; how many there are in a particular country or group, and what proportion of them are likely to be expensive; he can learn the order in which particular stamps were issued and the reason for them; he can find out which stamps he still needs to complete an issue.

But the collector who just studies the catalogue list and compares it with his collection is only half using the catalogue. Some of the catalogue's most interesting information is contained in the footnotes and explanations. Almost every collector *consults* the catalogue from time to time; I often think that we don't sit down and *read* it sufficiently often.

It is often said (and quite rightly) that to use an out-of-date catalogue is a false economy. But a volume of perhaps a thousand pages with many hundreds of illustrations obviously cannot be produced at a give-away price; and a second-hand catalogue, which is a year or two old, and which can often be picked up very cheaply, is certainly better than no catalogue at all. While it should be every collector's aim to secure a current catalogue of the stamps that interest him most as soon as possible, it is worth bearing in mind that up-to-date catalogues can usually be borrowed from public libraries – though you will probably have to reserve them. They may also be consulted at most reference libraries.

Gibbons is the only whole-world catalogue nowadays published in Britain. It is a world-renowned authority, especially for British Commonwealth issues. It is produced in two distinct versions: the full catalogue, and the *Stamps of the World* volume, formerly known as the Simplified.

For a long time now the *Stamps of the World* has been the only catalogue to list all the world's stamps in simplified form in one volume – and a hefty volume it is, too. As its former name implies, it is a very simple and straightforward catalogue; only the major colours are mentioned, no shades; there are no varieties of perforation or watermark (though imperforate stamps are distinguished), no minor differences in designs. As regards its pricing policy, the catalogue quotes a value for the commonest variety of each stamp. So it is a very handy volume indeed for the beginner or the 'simple life' collector who doesn't want anything too complicated and is more interested in stamp designs than in the more 'scientific' aspects of stamp lore.

Many years ago it was also possible to obtain the full Gibbons catalogue in a single volume, but the last edition to come out in that form was the 1940, compiled just before the war. Until 1970 it was published in three volumes – Part I covering the British Commonwealth; Part II dealing with Europe and colonies; and Part III for the rest of the world.

Now the publishers have announced a new policy. The British Commonwealth catalogue will continue to appear in one volume, but the rest of the world's stamps will be listed in a new sectionalised catalogue: a uniform series of paper-backs, each one dealing with a particular country or group. The first nine of these were published in September 1970, and the series was to be completed in September 1971. After that, new editions of the various sections would appear from time to time.

This method has two main advantages. It means that a collector need buy only those sections which especially interest him instead of a larger and more expensive volume; and each section, being a smaller task of publishing and printing, can be that much more up-to-date.

In addition there is the Elizabethan catalogue. This includes British Commonwealth stamps of the present reign only, repeating the Elizabethan lists from the British Commonwealth catalogue but with a certain amount of extra detail, notably minor shades.

Another noted British catalogue, which has many devoted adherents, is the Commonwealth. This is limited to stamps of the British Commonwealth only, and it appears in two volumes, which in recent years, curiously enough, have been put out by different publishers. The Commonwealth Queen Elizabeth Catalogue covers virtually the same field as the Elizabethan. The other volume, increasingly referred to as the Bridger and Kay (from its publishers), was formerly concerned with King George VI stamps only, but is now being progressively extended to earlier reigns. So before long it looks as though collectors will have the choice of two rival British Commonwealth catalogues, both published in this country – something they have not had since the once-famous Whitfield King catalogue appeared for the last time some twenty years ago.

It is unlikely that the beginner will encounter foreign catalogues for some time, but it is as well to know their names so that you will recognise them if you see or hear any reference to them. In America the leading catalogues are the old-established Scott's, and its newer rival, Minkus. In France the great authority is the Yvert catalogue; in West Germany it is the Michel. Another noted European catalogue is the Zumstein, published in Switzerland and printed in German. All these catalogues are known for being particularly detailed in certain sections. For instance the advanced collector of French stamps would certainly like to have the appropriate volume of Yvert on his desk as well as the French section of Gibbons.

The *Stamps of the World* will probably fill the general collector's needs for the first year or two, but it may not be long before his interest is aroused by the more technical side of the hobby. He will begin to realise that some stamps can be found in quite marked shades of colouring, on different kinds of paper, with small but interesting variations in the design, with different watermarks or different perforations.

And this will mean that some of the stamps he has hither-to regarded as duplicates can now be included in the collection as separate varieties, some of them, moreover, being of greater value than the basic stamp. This is the sort of information he will find by studying the full catalogue.

To indicate the difference between the two catalogues, let us take the somewhat obvious example of the early stamps of Great Britain . . . For the 1840 issue, the *Stamps of the World* illustrates the design and then follows the basic information: '1840. Letters in lower corners. Imperf.' (The note about letters in lower corners helps the collector to distinguish this issue from later ones with letters in all four corners.)

In contrast the full catalogue illustrates both the design and the small crown watermark found on this issue, and names the engraver and printers. The heading follows: '1840 (6 MAY). Letters in lower corners. Wmk. Small Crown. Imperf '

When we come to the actual list, the simplified volume gives '1d. black' and '2d. blue', and that's that. The full catalogue gives three shades of each, and then proceeds to list and price the various plate numbers of the Penny Black followed by twenty varieties on the Penny Black and fourteen on the Twopence Blue!

The simplified catalogue lists the basic issues of Great Britain from 1840 up to 1867 most concisely in just thirty stamps. The same period is covered in the full catalogue in one hundred and twenty stamps, plus a large number of the minor varieties in which specialists take much delight.

To save space, the simplified volume telescopes some issues, giving as the date of issue only the year in which the first stamp of the group happened to appear. Chrono-logically, as in so many other ways, the full catalogue is much more detailed.

Often the difference between the two catalogues is most noticeable among the earlier issues, in which much research has been carrried out over the years. The Great Britain list

43

of Gibbons British Commonwealth catalogue, in particular, is fairly highly specialized; so if this is regarded as a somewhat exaggerated example, let us tread a less frequented path to the first issue of Bolivia. Here the Gibbons sectionalised distinguishes six types of the first Condor design and these, with permutations of shades and colour changes, bring the list to a total of thirty-two stamps. The simplified volume dismisses this same issue in just seven!

Catalogues are usually arranged on more or less alphabetical lines by countries, but there are exceptions. Dependencies are often given after their mother countries. Recognised groups often appear together, such as the German States, preceding the main list of Germany. Then occupation issues, as a rule, are found listed after those of the occupying power, not with those of the actual country where they were used.

In doubtful cases, refer to the index. Please remember also to read the introduction to the catalogue with some care, noting especially the symbols used by the publishers. There is much helpful information for beginners in the introduction, and all too few collectors take the trouble to study it.

Although different catalogues vary quite considerably in scope and presentation, the general plan of most of them is similar, having stood the test of time. At the head of each issue comes one or more illustrations of the designs, each accompanied by a number in heavy type. This is called the type number and relates to the design, not to any particular stamp. With each type number normally appears a brief description of the design, unless the subject is so obvious as to make this unnecessary. Then may follow, at least in the more detailed publications, the printing process, names of designer, engraver and printers, and so on.

The list is headed by the date of issue, perhaps a note of any feature distinguishing the issue from those that precede or follow it, the occasion or purpose of the issue if commemorative, the watermark (if any) and the gauge of perforation.

Perforations are expressed in terms of a number, which is in fact the number of perforation holes in a length of two centimetres, a system invented back in 1866 by a Frenchman who chose this unit because he found that most stamps were about two centimetres wide. In a catalogue 'Perf. 14' therefore means that there are 14 perforation holes in every length of two centimetres all round the stamp.

In cases where the perforations do not measure the same all the way round, it is always the measurement across the top that is taken first. For many years now the great majority of British stamps have been 'Perf. 15 x 14'. This is known as a compound perforation, and means that there are 15 perforation holes to every two centimetres across the top and bottom, but 14 holes down each side.

Some collectors disdain to measure perforations, feeling that such things are beneath their notice, and of course that is their privilege. But in a number of cases a scarce perforation can add greatly to the value of a stamp, and from this aspect alone it seems worth paying some attention to them.

Changes of perforation during the currency of an issue still occur from time to time. Due to the stringency of wartime conditions there were many interesting perforation changes in British Commonwealth issues during the Second World War period. But such changes are much less frequent nowadays than in years gone by. We are unlikely to see in new issues the situation arising, for example, in the 1872–88 issue of the Netherlands, which can be found in five different varieties of perforation – still less the extreme of the 1867-80 stamps of Austria, with thirteen different perforations!

Resuming now our consideration of the catalogue, we come next to the actual list. On the left-hand side you will find a column of numbers. All the stamps of each country are numbered in sequence, starting from '1'. This is called the catalogue number, and is a useful device for identifying stamps easily without having to give a complete description. To quote numbers from the Stanley Gibbons catalogue, the initials 'S.G.' are prefixed. Thus 'Great Britain S.G. 700' indicates immediately to any collector at all acquainted with British stamps the 4d. stamp issued in August 1966 to commemorate England's football victory in the World Cup. This is simply because it happens to be No. 700 in the Gibbons list.

Reading across the line, next to the catalogue number comes the face value of the stamp, that is the value at which it was originally sold by the Post Office; then the colour or colours. In the case of brightly coloured modern issues the catalogue compilers have given up the unequal struggle when five or more colours are used on a single stamp, and now resort to 'multi-coloured'!

Finally there are two price columns: the left-hand one for unused stamps, the right-hand one for used. Do not jump to the conclusion that these prices are what your stamps are 'worth' – a common failing among new collectors! As I have already explained, they are the catalogue editor's opinion of a reasonable retail price for individual stamps in first-class condition at the time when the list was compiled or last revised. Moreover there must inevitably be a minimum catalogue price per stamp and in the case of Gibbons this is now as much as 5p, even for the commonest stamp. There are, of course, large numbers of stamps which are not worth anything like 5p, and probably never will. The catalogue publishers readily admit as much, stating that 5p in such cases must be regarded not as a price but as a 'handling charge'. In other words there is a price below which, costs being what they are, it does not pay a dealer to handle any individual stamp.

It's a great thrill when, for the first time, you look up a stamp in the catalogue and discover that it's a scarcer variety than you thought. Before claiming it as such, however, make very certain that you have read the catalogue correctly! Special care is needed when identifying what you hopefully consider to be a rare shade. In fact it is wiser not to try naming shades without other shades of the same stamp for comparison.

If you cannot find a stamp in the catalogue, it may be due to any one of several reasons. It may be a new issue, released after the catalogue went to press. It may be a fiscal, that is to say, a stamp used for revenue purposes and not valid for postage; it may even be a publicity label of some kind. Or it may be a 'local', a privately-issued stamp for some local post, not sponsored by the official post office and therefore outside the scope of the catalogue.

Before deciding that the stamp is not included, however, take a look at the end of the list of the country in question. You may have an official stamp (used by government departments) or a postage due, or some other special-purpose stamp listed separately from the others. In some cases you may also find that charity stamps are grouped together after the ordinary issues.

For advanced collectors, there are advanced catalogues. A goodly number of the more popular countries have highly specialized publications devoted to them. There are excellent catalogues of this kind covering the stamps of Great Britain, Australia, Switzerland, the United States, New Zealand, and many more. Then there are the scholarly (and expensive) volumes of the Encyclopaedia of British Empire Postage Stamps, published by Robson Lowe. In style these are a mixture of textbook and catalogue. Including as they do reference to the postal markings of the pre-stamp era, these valuable works are of special interest to postal historians.

CHAPTER FIVE

THE STORY OF THE POST

Stamps are fascinating things in themselves, but they become still more interesting when considered in the light of the wider subject of postal history. In the last thirty-five years in particular the hobby has acquired a new dimension.

Many collectors now study not only the stamps but the cancellations and the other postmarks on the envelope, and indeed the envelope itself. They want to know why a certain postal rate was paid, the route by which the letter travelled, the time it took on the journey, and so on. At the same time they are extending their collections back in point of time to the pre-stamp era, including covers and postmarks of those times in their albums as a prelude to the actual stamp collection.

Whether you become a keen postal historian or not, however, your appreciation of stamps will be enhanced if you understand at least a little of the history and development of the postal service, in which stamps have played such an important part.

When you stop to think about it, a stamp is one of the marvels of modern times. A stamp will convey your letter safely and speedily over oceans, mountains and political boundaries, to Frinton or Fiji, to Macclesfield, Madras or Melbourne and all at a cost within the reach of everyone. Despite the modern emphasis on the telephone and tele-communications, the progress of the whole world of commerce and industry still depends on the prompt and reliable transmission of the written word.

The efficiency of our world-wide post is nowadays taken so much for granted that we tend to overlook how relatively recent an institution it is. Postal services certainly existed for centuries before the postage stamp appeared, but it was the postage stamp that made them available to everyone.

How, then, did the story of the post begin? Cyrus the Great of Persia, in the 6th century B.C., is credited with having organised the first system of couriers to carry his messages and instructions to the distant parts of his empire. The Romans, with their natural flair for organisation, took up the idea with success, and the officials of the *Cursus publicus* were the first such messengers to carry an identifying device as a sign of their authority. This was a bronze tablet, which might be regarded as the earliest forerunner of the badge and uniform of the modern postman.

The Roman relay station where the messenger changed horses or handed over his dispatches was known as a *positus*, and from this term is descended the word 'post'. But this system, too, was for official documents only, and private citizens had to make their own arrangements.

In medieval times the royal courts arranged relays of couriers, but apart from these only the universities, the great religious orders and the wealthier merchants could afford to pay messengers to carry their letters.

In France, King Louis XI set up a regular postal service as early as 1461, and a few years later allowed the public to make use of it. It was so expensive that only the well-to-do could send their letters by this means, but even so an important principle had been established: a state-run enterprise for the benefit of anyone who was prepared to pay the postage. The bag in which the French courier carried the letters was called a *malle*, and from this the modern word 'mail' is derived.

Meanwhile the beginnings of the first international postal service could be detected. From a modest start in Italy towards the end of the 13th century, successive generations of the famous Thurn and Taxis family were developing a postal system which grew to cover a large part of

49

Europe. Early in the 16th century, Franz Taxis provided postal facilities throughout the Holy Roman Empire, France and Spain. At the time the scale of the enterprise was without precedent, but the Thurn and Taxis post not only honoured its commitments but rapidly extended them. By 1625, 20,000 couriers were employed on regular routes over the greater part of western and central Europe, and were noted for their speed and reliability.

It was the upheaval caused by the Napoleonic wars that led to the decline of the Thurn and Taxis post, but in parts of Germany it survived into the stamp era, issuing its own stamps from 1852 until the service was finally bought out by Prussia in 1867. The Thurn and Taxis issues, usually listed in the catalogues under German States, are therefore a unique link with the earliest days of organised public postal service in Europe.

In Britain the first postal facilities, as in other countries, were provided by a group of royal couriers who conveyed messages as and when required. But by the time of Henry VIII the service had become important enough for the first Master of the King's Post to be appointed. He was Sir Brian Tuke, and his main contribution to postal development was to establish regular schedules.

On pain of imprisonment, innkeepers were required to provide horses for the royal messengers for the next stage of their journey. To return the horse safely to its stable, the messenger was usually accompanied by a 'post boy', who carried private letters.

Three years after the defeat of the Spanish Armada, Elizabeth I tried to put a stop to any further foreign intrigue by commanding that all letters to and from foreign countries should be conveyed only by her official messengers – an interesting move because it anticipated the theory that the carriage of letters should be a state monopoly.

Not until 1635 were the posts made officially available for private mail. In that year Thomas Witherings, the Post-

50

master-General, set up the six great post roads: from London to Edinburgh, Plymouth, Bristol, Chester, Yarmouth and Dover, with branch routes (by-posts', they were called) to smaller towns.

On the Restoration of the monarchy in 1660, one Henry Bishop became Postmaster-General, and he has a secure niche in history as the inventor of the first postmark. In 1661 he announced: 'A stamp is invented that is putt upon every letter showing the day of the moneth that every letter comes to the office, so that no Letter Carrier may dare detayne a letter from post to post, which before was usual.'

The postmark was one of Bishop's ideas for improving the service in response to public criticism! It consisted simply of the first two letters of the month and the date within a small circle. It is worth noting however, that Bishop described it as a 'stamp' and this, of course, was the original meaning of the word: a handstamp used to impress a postal marking on a letter. Indeed, when adhesive postage stamps first came out, they were described by the Post Office as labels! Just as a further complication, the term label means to a modern collector not a postage stamp but any other kind of sticker without postal validity. The early postmarks are known as 'Bishop marks', after their inventor.

In 1680 a merchant, William Dockwra, started the first local penny post, a private venture covering London and its suburbs. It was also the first service to use postmarks indicating that postage had been prepaid – thus serving a similar purpose to postage stamps. With its cheap, flat rates of postage and its frequent door-to-door deliveries, Dockwra's system was a remarkable precursor of modern postal facilities. It was so successful that within two years a legal action was brought against the proprietor for infringement of the state postal monopoly, whereupon the service was promptly taken over by the government!

The Bishop marks and the triangular 'Penny Post Paid' markings of Dockwra's post were in a very real sense the ancestors of the stamps and postmarks in use today. The other element of modern postmarks, the town of dispatch, came along rather later, 18th century examples including the mileage from London. This information was required because the rates of postage differed according to the distance which the letter travelled.

A big fault of the system in the early days was that all letters originating on one of the great post roads and destined for a place on one of the others had to pass through London. Thus a letter, say, from Plymouth to Bristol had to travel to the London G.P.O. and then out again, instead of going direct. To overcome this delay Ralph Allen, postmaster at Bath, suggested a system of cross-country postal routes and these, known as cross posts, first came into operation in 1720.

By a coincidence the next great advance also originated from Bath. John Palmer was a theatrical manager in that city whose business frequently took him to London. He could not help contrasting the speed of the stage-coach with that of the humble post-boy, plodding along on horseback at the regulation speed of four miles an hour. He put forward a scheme for the introduction of mail coaches. The idea received strong support from William Pitt, the Prime Minister, and Britain's first mail coach left Bristol for London in August 1784. Before long the mail coach network had spread to most of the major towns of the country, making use of the road improvements effected by the turnpike trusts.

For half a century the mail coaches were queens of the road. But then, with dramatic suddenness, their heyday ended with the coming of the railways. In remoter districts, however, they continued to operate for a number of years after most of the trunk railways had been constructed. The last one, in the north of Scotland, survived until 1874.

Meanwhile, in 1773, penny posts similar to that operating in London were opened in Dublin and Edinburgh, and afterwards in a steadily growing number of other towns. These offered a good service for local letters, but for mail over a longer distance the system still left much to be desired.

The main grievance was the high cost of postage, and moreover the rates were increased from time to time. A single-sheet letter sent from London to a town a hundred miles distant, for example, cost 4d. in 1711, 5d. in 1784, 6d. in 1796, 7d. in 1801, 8d. in 1805, and 9d. in 1812.

Although postage could be paid by the sender – in which case a red postmark would be applied instead of a black one – the usual practice was to collect payment from the addressee. Postage rates varied not only according to the distance the letter travelled, but according to the number of sheets of paper which it comprised. It was a complicated system which was open to wide-spread abuse, notably arising from the privilege of free postage granted to members of Parliament. In fact the free letters usually greatly outnumbered the ones that were paid for.

Such a system might have sufficed while letter-writing was limited mainly to the nobility and gentry, but these were changing times. The onset of the Industrial Revolution brought a great increase in industrial and commercial activity, and with it growing pressure for a speedier, more efficient and above all cheaper postal service.

So the stage was set for the great reforms brought about by Sir Rowland Hill. His early experiences in helping to colonise South Australia convinced him of the urgent need for simplifying and reducing the complex postage rates then in force. From his investigations he calculated that the high cost of postage arose not from the expense of conveying the mail but from the colossal amount of time and effort devoted to sorting the paid from the unpaid letters and working out the amount of postage due, and then to the time-consuming procedure of collecting the money. If all this clerical work could be avoided, he believed that postal

53

rates could be substantially reduced. He expounded his views in a celebrated pamphlet published in 1837, and two years later he was attached to the Treasury to put his reforms into practice.

The system which he introduced was indeed a postal revolution. The first principle was that all postage should be prepaid by the sender. The second was the adoption of a uniform rate of postage on all letters within the U.K., irrespective of the distance they travelled. The third was the abolition of the free postage privilege. On 5th December 1839, an experimental flat rate of 4d. per letter was introduced, and on 10th January 1840 the rate was reduced to 1d. For a few months more the postage had to be paid over the post counter in cash, until the world's first postage stamps were ready on 6th May. The Penny Black was intended for letters up to half-ounce in weight; the Twopence Blue was for letters between half an ounce and one ounce.

They appeared at the same time as the first prepaid postal stationery – envelopes and letter-sheets which have become known to collectors as Mulreadies, so called after William Mulready, the artist who designed them. But to the surprise of Sir Rowland Hill the postal stationery was a flop from the first. The designs proved unpopular and were soon caricatured. (The caricatures are today much prized as collector's pieces!) No, it was the stamps which the British public promptly took to their hearts – the convenient, adhesive postage stamps which Hill had added to his scheme, almost as an afterthought, as an alternative for those who insisted on using their own writing paper!

Critics of this bold scheme forecast that it would never pay. To some extent one can understand their forebodings. To some, the idea of reducing the postage on a single-sheet letter from London to Edinburgh from 1s. 1½d. to 1d. must indeed have seemed too good to be true! But that is what happened. For the first year or two, the total postal revenue

54

was certainly much less than in pre-stamp times, but in the longer term Hill's confidence in the economics of his reforms was fully justified.

Commercially and socially, the benefits of uniform penny postage were immense. In 1846, the sum of £13,000 was raised by public subscription and presented to Hill as a public benefactor. The effect of his reforms was to raise the number of inland letters from about 77 millions in 1838 to 642 millions by the time he retired in 1864. Few individuals, probably, have added so much to the total of human happiness and prosperity.

The advent of cheap postage coincided with the railway age, which itself speeded up the transport of the mails. Prior to the 1840's, the majority of people lived in a narrow world, never sending or receiving letters and rarely moving far away from their native villages or towns. The railways and cheap postage brought a greater degree of freedom and mobility to the man-in-the-street than he had ever known before – and with these two commercial advantages the Victorians were ready to lead Britain into the forefront of world affairs.

Perhaps, after all, it is not so surprising that stamps attracted the attention of collectors at such an early date. The Victorians appreciated stamps for what they were: symbols of a social as well as an industrial revolution.

To cope with the growth of postal traffic all sorts of improvements and refinements have been added since Hill's time, but the soundness of his reforms is shown by the fact that today, more than one hundred and thirty years later, we are collecting stamps of similar shape and size, stamps which fulfil exactly the same purpose, as those which first appeared in 1840.

CHAPTER SIX

ALBUMS AND ACCESSORIES

After acquiring some stamps, your next stage is to find something to put them in, and this brings us to the subject of albums. It would, I suppose, still be possible to enjoy stamp collecting if you put your stamps in a notebook or just kept them loose in envelopes. But most collectors take some pride in their stamps and like to arrange them neatly in an album where they can be easily inspected and are protected from loss or damage.

Cheap albums for the beginner can be bought for only a few new pence, and many are really excellent value, perhaps including a series of coloured maps to help you to locate the less well-known stamp-issuing countries. Their disadvantage is that they usually provide for stamps to be mounted on both the left-hand and right-hand pages, with the result that stamps may get caught up with one another, and perhaps even torn, if the album is opened in a hurry. Nevertheless, one of these cheap albums will make a convenient home for the stamps you have sorted from your large mixed packets and any others you may have obtained from the mail.

Albums of this sort have the country names, and perhaps a few other details, printed at the top of the page, with one or two illustrations of stamps. The pages are divided into rectangles of dotted lines, inside which stamps may be mounted, although these are less help then they used to be because quite a number of modern stamps are in unconventional shapes and sizes.

Of course you mustn't expect too much from a small, fast-bound album. When you bear in mind that there are today well over two hundred countries, large and small, currently issuing stamps (to say nothing of the numerous 'dead' countries) it will be obvious that there cannot be a whole page for each one. And while more space will be allocated to those countries most likely to be strongly represented in a beginner's collection, it is inevitable that before long some pages will become overcrowded while others remain bare.

The next step, therefore, is an album that has leaves similarly printed, but only the right-hand pages, and is also of greater capacity and loose-leaf – with a spring-back binder so that extra leaves can be added and re-arranged as desired. There are several good-quality albums of this type on the market, providing handy accommodation for the 'bit of everything' collection up to two thousand stamps or more. Extra leaves can be bought in packets quite cheaply, and it's a good idea to get at least one packet when you buy the album. It is also worth remembering that the pages for which you have no stamps at present can be removed from the binder until they are needed.

Such an album offers a certain degree of flexibility as your collection begins to grow, and you can begin to arrange your stamps in some sort of order. But don't try to force too many additional pages into the binder or the spring may suddenly snap and you will find your entire collection scattered over the table or the floor!

Another kind of printed album is the descendant of the old-time album described in the first chapter, with each stamp identified and a definite space allotted for it. Generally, albums of this type are nowadays intended for collections of a specific period – for issues up to 1936, for example, or the stamps of King George VI only. The reason for this is clear. With the large numbers of new issues appearing every year, such an album would so quickly become out-of-date if it attempted to cover more modern material.

In the last few years, however, there has been an interesting development of this idea which caters for the one-country enthusiast. A series of albums has appeared on the market, very attractive productions, which are devoted to one (or occasionally more than one) of the more popular British Commonwealth countries. Just like grandfather's albums they have spaces allotted for every stamp up to the date of printing, but they are also loose-leaf so that additional material or new issues can be inserted on extra leaves. They sell at around two pounds each, and for a collector who hasn't the time or inclination to devote much effort to arranging and writing-up his collection, they really offer the best of both worlds!

But in most cases, sooner or later, the collection, the knowledge and the enthusiasm of the collector outgrow the limitations of a printed album and he graduates to the plain, loose-leaf album which permits a more personalised kind of stamp collecting. In these, the leaves are devoid of printing except for a pale grey quadrille network which serves as a guide for mounting.

The collector will find a wide choice awaiting him. He can select anything from a simple, spring-back binder containing fifty or one hundred unembellished but perfectly adequate leaves to a sumptuous leather bound volume with an elaborate mechanism and expensive, linen-hinged leaves. It is said with truth that a good collection deserves a good album, but obviously it is also wise to have some regard to the standard of collection that a new album is likely to house! Other things being equal, it is advisable to choose a fairly well known album from a fairly well known maker, if only because you are then most likely to be able to obtain further volumes to match it, as well as extra leaves, without difficulty.

Leaves are made in a range of standard sizes. The one most often seen which is very suitable for the great majority of collections measures $8\frac{5}{8}$ in. wide by $10\frac{3}{8}$ in., the overall album size being about 9 in. by 11 in. including the spring-back. But there are some larger ones for those who prefer them, as well as a number of smaller ones which may be useful for 'sideline' collections.

Many leaves are fluted down the left-hand side; this is to enable the spring-back binder to grip them more securely. You can also obtain black leaves instead of white. These display stamps to extremely good effect, but make writing-up more difficult. The beginner may find some significance in the fact that the majority of advanced collectors still prefer to stick to white leaves.

Apart from spring-backs, there are ring-fitting and peg-fitting loose-leaf albums. These are usually rather more expensive, and they do not always hold the leaves quite so rigidly as a spring-back, but their great advantage is that the album always lies quite flat at whatever page it is opened. The ring-fitting album is perhaps the easiest of all for removing or replacing leaves.

In the first chapter I mentioned that one of the blessings of stamp collecting is that it does not require complicated and costly equipment. I have already discussed the importance of the catalogue in the philatelic scheme of things, and when you have an album and a catalogue the only other accessory which is really essential rather then merely desirable is some stamp hinges.

Is it still necessary, in this day and age, to warn people not to stick stamps down in the album with stamp edging or other adhesive paper? This certainly happened all too often in the old days. Some of the early collectors used paste and even glue to fix their stamps into the album – apparently determined that they should never come out again – and one shudders to think of the number of fine stamps that were ruined in the process. Even the commonest stamps deserve careful mounting with good quality hinges.

With stamp hinges it pays to buy the best, and they are not expensive. A thousand excellent hinges can be bought for about 10p. As soon as you have taken them home, I suggest you put them in a small tin, which is so much more convenient for keeping hinges up together than the original packet, which inevitably gets torn. Hinges are doubly gummed, thin pieces of almost transparent paper; and when the time comes for the collection to be remounted, a hinge should, with care, peel easily from both stamp and album leaf, leaving little or no mark on either. The method of mounting will be described in the next chapter.

After hinges there are a few small items which may usefully be added to the collector's outfit. First among these I would place tweezers. Some beginners may think that tweezers are just an unnecessary fad. You may feel that tweezers are all very well for learned collectors handling rare stamps with the same care they would devote to diamonds (as well they might!) but hardly for lesser mortals. You may add that in any case you would never contemplate handling stamps without scrupulously clean hands.

Maybe so, but the cleanest hands can be warm and slightly moist, and repeated handling with the fingers will certainly not do stamps any good, especially unused ones. True, it may not be so important when you have only very common stamps in your collection, but it is as well to begin the way you mean to continue.

Quite apart from this question of protection, tweezers have another practical advantage. With a little practice you will find it much easier and quicker to pick up and examine stamps with the aid of tweezers and before long you will wonder how you ever managed without them!

An average pair of chromium-plated tweezers, obtainable for about 40p, will last a lifetime. You can choose between round-shaped and spade-shaped ends. Make sure they don't have any sharp edges which could harm your stamps. A useful tip is to pick up a plain sheet of paper with them and see if they leave any mark behind. I assume that everyone realises that I am here writing of philatelic tweezers made for the job, and not the eyebrow-plucking variety!

A magnifier could be the next item on the collector's

shopping list. There are some splendid battery-operated illuminated magnifiers on the market, which are the ideal way of examining stamps in detail. Some of these cost less than £1, though others are a good deal more expensive. To carry around with you, a small pocket magnifier, with its own case, costs only a few new pence and will be quite sufficient for most collector's needs.

As your collection advances, you will be introduced to watermarks and perforations, and here too there are several useful accessories to help. Watermarks are best examined from the back of the stamp. Some show up quite easily; others are much more difficult to see. It helps to put the stamp face down on a black surface, and small trays are available for this purpose. If the watermark is still reluctant to appear, a drop or two of benzine poured on to it will do the trick. Your dealer will be able to supply you with benzine, a highly volatile liquid, in a small bottle conveniently equipped with a stopper of the 'dropper' type. As an alternative, and particularly for some modern photogravure stamps which may not take kindly to benzine, a battery-operated electric watermark detector, which operates on a system of coloured filters, is most effective: quicker and easier than the other method, but also more expensive.

To measure perforations you will require a perforation gauge. Simple card gauges, about the size of a postcard, can be obtained for this purpose. On the card is printed a series of rows of dots at varying distances apart – each row with the appropriate number. You place the perforations of your stamp along each row until you find one that exactly matches the perforation holes and the number alongside gives the gauge of the stamp.

A snag of this type of gauge is that it is not easy to use on stamps which are mounted in an album or are still on the original cover. For the past twenty years or so, however, another kind of gauge has been available which overcomes this difficulty. Known as the 'Instanta', it is engraved on transparent plastic, and it uses a system of converging lines. The collector simply slides the gauge up and down until the perforation holes of the stamp coincide with the lines, and then reads the gauge from the scale printed at the side. With the 'Instanta' advanced collectors can even read perforations to a decimal point if they wish to do so.

A problem often encountered by a beginner in stamp-collecting relates to colour. The colours and shades of stamps are keenly studied, so it is helpful if you know, in your mind's eye, the difference between purple, violet, lilac and mauve, between emerald green and turquoise-green, between claret and cerise. The accepted nomenclature of philatelic colours differs from colour names in other parts of life. It is no use looking at a paint manufacturer's colour card, for example, and expecting to find the same names attributed to the same colours in a stamp catalogue.

Knowledge of stamp colours often comes with experience. But even experienced collectors sometimes find it difficult to name an isolated colour on sight. So why not buy a colour guide? This gives the one hundred colours most widely used in stamp identification. Bear in mind that the guide gives solid blocks of colour, so compare them with the most solid part of the stamp design. It is curious how the eye can be misled about a colour when seen only in a lightly shaded part of the stamp.

A duplicate book is another accessory worth consideration. There are many sizes – from the slim booklet to slip into the pocket, to a hefty volume of such capacity and quality as to rival (and outclass!) most dealers' stock books. Quite different from an album, the pages of a duplicate book have horizontal slots, often made of transparent material, in which loose stamps may be placed. Stamps are thus kept safe and sound, and can be arranged at will in countries or sets, until such time as they are disposed of (if they are duplicates) or mounted in the album (if they are new acquisitions).

The really keen collector, of course, is never without his duplicate book. Usually he also has about his person a small notebook listing his 'wants'. After all, you never know when someone may offer you a stamp! But please, never decline it because it doesn't happen to be what you are collecting just at present. This one may be a poor thing, but refuse it and the donor will never offer you another, whereas the next one may be a very good stamp indeed! So thank him warmly, slip the stamp into your duplicate book, and examine it at your leisure – even if it is only to pass it on to another collector.

Yes, the duplicate book is a useful article. But when it comes to sorting large quantities of stamps it is not always big enough. In this case a few small envelopes are as good as anything. The glassine envelopes in which dealers sell stamps to you are worth keeping for this very purpose!

When all our philatelic accessories have been considered, it remains true that a collector with two or three albums can keep the lot, with his catalogue and other aids, in a fair-sized desk drawer. There are not many hobbies of which *that* can be said!

As a general rule, however, it is better to keep albums upright on a shelf. Stamps are best stored in a dry atmosphere, and albums should be opened to 'air' the stamps occasionally. As long-term advice, watch out for any signs of 'foxing' on your album leaves – those brownish marks which sometimes appear on the page edges of old books and so on. The stamps on any leaves which become thus affected should be remounted as soon as possible.

CHAPTER SEVEN

PREPARING AND ARRANGING THE COLLECTION

While you are using a beginner's printed album, even the loose-leaf variety, the scope for presenting a collection to its best advantage is severely limited. Little more can be done than arrange sets in the right order and issues in broadly the correct date sequence.

But as soon as you move on to a blank leaf album the opportunities for individual initiative in displaying your stamps are endless. There are probably as many ways of arranging a collection as there are collectors and this chapter must be confined to a few ideas which the majority have found helpful by experience.

First of all there is the question of preparing stamps for the album. Some, for example, may have bits of the envelope still adhering to them. It goes without saying, I hope, that you will first make sure that you will not be destroying any-thing interesting in the way of postmarks before deciding to remove the paper. Having done this, how do you set about the job?

One method is by floating the stamps on the surface of a saucer of water, until the moisture is absorbed by the paper and the stamps can be peeled off easily. But take care not to let the water get on the surface of the stamp where it may cause damage, especially to modern issues. An alternative is to rest the items (stamp face upwards, of course) on several thicknesses of wet blotting paper. There are also 'sweat-boxes' on the market which serve a similar purpose.

To attempt to remove a stamp from paper without adopting one of these methods is liable to result in disaster, but if you must try it, choose common stamps and never pull the stamp from the paper. Always turn it over and peel the paper from the stamp.

The importance of using good quality hinges has already been stressed. When starting to mount stamps, first remove the leaves from the album. Fold over no more than a quarter of the hinge, gummed side outwards, making sure that the fold is straight, very slightly moisten this top quarter and affix it to the top of the back of the stamp, just below the top perforations. Then lightly moisten the other part of the hinge at its lower edge, and fix this to the album leaf. Only the slightest moistening is required, and by taking care over this operation – and using tweezers, of course – it will be possible to remount the stamp later on, if desired, without causing the stamp any damage and using the same hinge.

All this is straightforward enough where used stamps are concerned, but as regards unused, the hobby has been affected in the last few years by the craze for 'unmounted mint'. This is followed by those who consider that a stamp can no longer be truly regarded as mint when once it has been sullied by a hinge, however lightly and correctly employed. They like their stamps to be entirely unmarked and unmounted – but in that case how do you put them in an album? The answer is by protective mounts, formerly known as pochettes and usually referred to by their trade name of Hawid strips.

These are folders, obtainable in a full range of sizes including large ones for blocks of stamps or covers, with a transparent front and a back of solid colour, frequently black. The stamps are just placed in the folder where they remain attractively displayed, instantly available for inspection, but completely protected. The Hawid Strip can then itself be mounted (with one hinge at each end) to the album leaf, or actually gummed to it.

Unfortunately the system of protective mounts is rather

expensive, and in the case of a beginner the cost of the mount may approach the cost of the stamps inside it! It may be said that this modern insistence on mint stamps being unhinged is another reason for preferring to collect used.

If you feel that this is taking 'condition mania' to somewhat extravagant lengths, you are not alone in that opinion. But when dealers advertising to buy stamps frequently stipulate that they will pay less for lightly hinged material than for unmounted mint, I can only recommend you, however reluctantly, not to mount your mint stamps with hinges, or at least those which have cost more than a few pence each.

The unmounted mint vogue first became apparent in the early 1960s. It is all very well for modern issues of the past decade, but what happens when a collector who has grown accustomed to insisting on unmounted mint turns his attention to issues more than ten or fifteen years old? Stocks of such stamps in unmounted mint condition just don't exist, and the only way that dealers can replenish their stocks of such material is from existing collections which come on to the market from time to time, and these are inevitably hinged. If anyone imagines that he will be able to obtain these older stamps at a substantial discount just because they have been mounted once, he is going to be rapidly disappointed!

Be that as it may, a cheaper though more laborious method than Hawid strips, which at least ensures that a mint stamp need never be hinged more than once, is to mount each stamp on a piece of colour-fast black paper or very thin card which has been cut to a suitable size – say one-eighth of an inch larger than the stamp all round. Such a card, known as a 'mat', is then itself mounted on the album leaf in the usual way. Then if any rearrangement or transfer is ever required, the mat is easily removed without disturbing the stamp or its precious coating of gum.

It is now time to consider the best arrangement of your

stamps in the album. Every collection is more interesting, both to the owner and to anyone else who may examine it, if a little thought and care are given to its presentation.

The quadrille-ruled background of the album leaf will help you to make sure that your stamps are mounted straight, and are placed at equal distances apart. But it is better to arrange matters so that stamps 'stand' on a line rather than 'hang' from it.

Again, the most methodical collectors may prefer to marshal their stamps in uniform rows, like soldiers on parade, but to my way of thinking it looks more attractive to achieve a pleasing balance of uneven rows, preferably with the shorter rows towards the foot of the page. For example, if you have sixteen equal-sized stamps to arrange on one album leaf, try putting them in rows of four, five, four and three, rather than in four rows of four. It is advisable to leave at least two, preferably three or four rows of quadrille squares horizontally between stamps, and rather more space, four or five squares, between rows.

Try not to overcrowd the pages. Thirty stamps should be regarded as the absolute maximum for an average-sized leaf; many collectors would put the figure a good deal lower than that! This not only creates a better appearance; it saves time and trouble in the long run by leaving space to add further stamps to the display as you acquire them.

Other things being equal, it is usual to arrange stamps in order of face value, the lowest first, as the catalogue does. This is convenient because it allows the higher values, which are often of larger size, to appear to good effect towards the foot of the page. Some modern issues, however, contain a fine assortment of shapes and sizes within the same set. In these cases it is better to ignore the sequence of face value and devise, by process of experiment, an arrangement which is aesthetically pleasing even if it means putting the higher values first!

In addition to offering the collector full rein for his

individual preferences as regards arrangement, the blank-leaf album also introduces him to the question of writing-up. Obviously a certain amount of description is necessary or the collection would convey very little. The barest minimum, I suppose, would be the year and purpose of the issue. When you reach the stage of devoting the whole of one album to the stamps of a single country, even the name of the country of origin would be scarcely necessary. But then, of course, if you feel inclined, you can devise a title page on which your artistic temperament can run riot!

Over and above this, the amount of detail that can be given depends entirely on the collector's interests (and knowledge) and the style of his collection. The catalogue provides most of the basic details, but although the catalogue makes a splendid servant there is no need to let it become your master. While it is a good idea to identify different watermarks and perforations where they exist, and to draw attention to any special items, it should be remembered that this is after all a stamp collection and the amount of description should not be so great as to overshadow the actual stamps. For the same reason excessive use of decoration and colour is better avoided.

Few of us are highly skilled in the art of penmanship, but this need not deter us from writing-up our collections. Many a fine collection has been most effectively presented in block capitals or the ordinary handwriting of the owner; I have even seen some quite advanced collections written-up in pencil! Of course, beautifully-shaped copperplate is pleasanter to the eye than careless scribble, but it is the content of the annotation that really matters more than its artistry.

For those whose ambitions lie in this direction, and who wish to delve into the technical aspects of manuscript styles especially suitable for stamp albums, there is an excellent book on the subject: *How to Arrange and Write Up a Stamp Collection*, by Stanley Phillips and C. P. Rang, published by Stanley Gibbons. The fact that this book has run through a number of editions and reprintings is a commendation in itself, and shows the interest taken in this side of the hobby.

If you are a poor calligrapher but a good typist, your writing-up can be typewritten. This method, it seems to me, detracts a little from the personal quality of the collection, but at least it has the advantage of complete legibility! With a typewriter, of course, each album leaf must be completely written-up before any stamps are mounted. As another alternative, one of the various stencilling outfits now on the market can provide very attractive results, though this method requires practice and takes time.

Worth consideration if you do not contemplate writing-up in great detail are the ready-gummed labels, printed with country headings and other standard philatelic information, which are readily obtainable. Another accessory, which can be most effective if used sparingly, consists of gummed paper arrows. These can be used for pointing out a variety on a stamp or some particular feature of a map, and so on.

I know of one collector, whose other hobby is printing, who has actually written-up (or perhaps 'printed-up' would be a better expression) his entire collection on his own printing press!

In specialized collections the quantity of writing-up will naturally be greater, aided perhaps by enlarged photographs or sketches of stamp designs. Similarly in postal history collections more writing-up is acceptable (and indeed desirable) to explain the significance of the material, including the postal rates and routes concerned. For beginners, however, a sensible general rule is to limit writing-up to the minimum consistent with the purpose of the collection. In particular catalogue numbers are an intrusion: catalogue prices even more so!

To avoid the risk of wasting any leaves, it is helpful to decide quite definitely what stamps are to appear and where, and then to add the writing-up very faintly in pencil, before starting work in earnest. This will also help to make sure that the written details as well as the stamps are symmetrically placed. If you do make a mistake, and mount a stamp in the wrong place, always remember to wait until the gum of the hinge is thoroughly dry before removing it. It should then peel away easily without damage.

A poorly arranged, overcrowded collection looks a dreary jumble; a well arranged, neatly written-up collection, on the other hand, is a source of pride to its owner, and can give pleasure and interest to his friends as well – possibly even encouraging them to become collectors too.

Even if for no other reason, it pays to give some attention to the arrangement of the collection, because when the stamps are assembled in reasonable order and are clearly identified, it helps to make sure that nothing worth while is overlooked when, in the fullness of time, the collector or his relatives come to dispose of the collection.

To learn the art of arrangement and writing up there is no better way than to visit as many stamp exhibitions as possible and study how other collectors tackle it. An hour or so at an exhibition, even if it is only a small local one arranged by the philatelic society in your own town, will be time well spent in many ways, and not least in the ideas you will pick up for arranging your own collection.

CHAPTER EIGHT

IDENTIFYING DIFFICULT STAMPS

With a little experience, most stamps are identified easily enough. Stamps of the British Commonwealth, for example, almost always carry the name of the issuing country in English, even though in some cases, such as Canada, India, Ceylon and Cyprus, it may appear in other languages too. (There are more stamps inscribed in two or three languages than you may think – another interesting philatelic byway.)

It is in the foreign section that the beginner is more likely to encounter problems of identification. And even if you have decided to collect only Australia and New Zealand, this is still a question that concerns you because as a keen collector you will never refuse a stamp – any stamp – when it is offered. Even if you don't intend to keep it you will still wish to identify it, to extend your philatelic knowledge, before disposing of it in exchange for a stamp that you do want.

Among the mystery stamps that do not at once proclaim their origin, let us first consider the 'mute' stamps – those that do not name the country of issue at all. (The term 'mute', by the way, is also applied to that small but interesting group of stamps which carry no expression of the face value).

Great Britain itself comes into this category. Sir Rowland Hill didn't think it necessary to include the name of the country on the first stamps. After all, there were no others in existence to be confused with them and in any case they were not going to be valid for postage on mail sent overseas! And the tradition has continued ever since – the head of the sovereign being considered sufficient identification.

It is a common falacy, however, to suppose that Britain is the only country with 'anonymous' stamps. The cantonal issues of Zurich and Geneva in Switzerland were the first to bear the name of the issuing authority in 1843; but the stamps of Brazil, which first appeared in the same year – the so-called 'bulls'-eyes' with their numeral design on a nearly-circular device – were mute, and so were all Brazilian stamps until 1866.

The early Brazilian issues were among the few with a numeral to indicate the value but no lettering of any kind. Even the Penny Black bore the words 'Postage' and 'One Penny', and one finds the equivalent in the early stamps of other nations. In the 1850s, Spain issued stamps with the word 'Correos' ('Postage'), but without the name of the country; likewise there were early mute stamps of Portugal, where the term is 'Correio', Denmark with 'Frimarke', Norway with 'Frimaerke', and the Netherlands with 'Postzegal'. Uruguay used 'Diligencia' on its first stamps, meaning 'Mailcoach', the method by which the mails were carried.

Turkish stamps divide themselves into two distinct periods. On those of the old Ottoman Empire, the only means of identification is the 'toughra', a device representing the stylised signature of the Sultan, which served a purpose somewhat comparable to that of the features of the monarch on British stamps. Modern Turkish issues, with the inscription 'Türkiye', are clear enough.

Great Britain apart, mute stamps are found mainly among the older material, but several countries make a regular practice of abbreviating their names to initials, providing another means of mystifying the beginner. Stamps inscribed 'RSA' (Republic of South Africa) have already been mentioned. 'U.S. Postage' will be recognised readily enough as emanating from the United States. Another example is France, most of whose stamps carry only the letters 'R.F.' (Republique Française). Up to 1958

Egyptian stamps were promptly identified by the name of the country in French or English, but since then this has been replaced by the initials, 'U.A.R.', standing for United Arab Republic. The stamps of the Soviet Union are easily distinguished by the initials 'CCCP'.

A case of unusual interest is the early issues of Palestine, a region which up to the end of the First World War was part of the Ottoman Empire. These show the initials 'E.E.F.', standing for Egyptian Expeditionary Force, and were first issued in 1918. The word Palestine did not make its bow on stamps until two years later, and even then only as an overprint on the E.E.F. stamps. Stamps inscribed Palestine did not appear until 1927.

In Europe, many of the country names on stamps are quite similar to the English equivalent, and so should not present much difficulty. For instance Belgique is clearly Belgium, Espana is Spain, Nederland is the Netherlands, Danmark is Denmark, and so on. It doesn't require great powers of deduction to work out that Romania or Posta Romana means Roumania, or that Polska is Poland or that Ccskoslovensko is Czechoslovakia. Not quite so obvious, perhaps, are Norge (or Noreg) for Norway, Sverige for Sweden, Island for Iceland, Lietuva for Lithuania and Eesti for Estonia.

Quite unlike the English names, in contrast, are Suomi (Finland) and Shqipenia and other similar names (Albania). Deutsches Reich, Reichspost and Deutsche Post all stand for Germany; nowadays West German stamps are inscribed Deutsche Bundespost, whereas East German issues are identified by Deutsche Demokratische Republik. Magyar stands for Hungary, and Osterreich for Austria.

Switzerland is a case on its own. This is a multi-lingual country, and so to avoid having to give the name several times over the 'neutral' Roman name of Helvetia appears on all the stamps.

In eastern Europe the collector encounters strange alphabets. Greek stamps are not too difficult, as the inscription ΕΛΛΑΣ (Hellas), or the abbreviation ΕΛΛ is soon recognised. The Cyrillic alphabet, seen on stamps of Russia, Yugoslavia and Bulgaria (and associated countries), is similar to the Greek in some respects, but can be quickly identified by such characters as the reversed 'R' and 'N'. In recent years both Yugoslavia and Bulgaria have come to the rescue of English-speaking collectors by adding the national name in Roman characters, while Soviet Russian issues, as already stated, present no problem.

It is not difficult to recognise Russian stamps of the Czarist era as most of them feature the imperial coat-of-arms. Some stamps of Finland are very similar to these but can usually be distinguished by the currency, expressed in 'penni' (frequently abbreviated to 'pen') and 'markaa'.

Stamps from Arabic countries are easier than you might suppose, because most modern stamps from this part of the world include the country's name in English as well as Arabic. If you find one that doesn't, try looking for it in the catalogue under Saudi Arabia – though even here, in recent years, we find the additional, fairly obvious, French inscription, Arabie Saoudite.

Persian stamps are identified either by the alternative name of Iran or by the French inscription, Postes Persanes. If you have a stamp in an unknown script which is neither Arabic nor Far Eastern, you may well locate it in one of the Indian Native States. None of these issue stamps any longer, but in days gone by they were responsible for some of the most primitive looking specimens ever mounted in an album. A few of them have a faint resemblance at first sight to odd scraps of blotting paper!

Turning to the Far East, most of the countries of southeast Asia are good enough to put their English names on the stamps. Remember, however, that Siam often appears by the alternative name of Thailand. Chinese stamps, up to the 1920s, are similarly easy to identify. But among the subsequent Chinese issues, and all the Japanese, the collector must find his way through a welter of oriental script. Japanese stamps up to 1947, however, are simple to recognize because all of them included in the design the circular chrysanthemum motif with its sixteen petals, the emblem of the Japanese royal family. Chinese stamps can often be distinguished either by the currency in cents or dollars, or by the oft-recurring portraits of Dr Sun Yat Sen and General Chiang Kai-shek; on the more modern issues, Chairman Mao is prominent. Otherwise a careful perusal of the illustrations and descriptions in the catalogue is the only sure guide.

Another group which sometimes causes a little confusion comprises those countries which have been known by different names during the stamp era. I have already mentioned in passing the new nations of Africa which come into this category, such as Ghana, Zambia, Botswana and Lesotho, still better known to many British collectors as Gold Coast, Northern Rhodesia, Bechuanaland and Basuto-land. One of these has actually issued stamps under three names: first British Central Africa, then Nyasaland, now Malawi. All three, be it noted, are the same place!

But certain countries outside Africa have also changed their names. Siam and Persia I have already referred to in this connection. Tasmania once issued stamps as Van Diemen's Land. Papua's early stamps were inscribed British New Guinea. Jordan was formerly known as Transjordan. Colombia's early stamps came out under the auspices of New Granada and the Granada Confederation.

We return to Africa, however, for perhaps the strangest problem of stamp identification: two countries with exactly the same name! Both the former French Congo and the former Belgian Congo have issued stamps inscribed Republique du Congo. For the beginner without a close acquaintance with these issues, reference to the catalogue is the only means of telling which is which. But latterly the former Belgian Congo has gone over to Republique Democratique du Congo – a distinction which stamp collectors must surely welcome!

Study your catalogue, and before long you will find little difficulty in identifying practically all the stamps that come your way, not just by the inscriptions on them but by the subjects and style of the designs. Certainly in modern times stamp recognition is becoming easier as English is increasingly accepted as the international language and nations the world over wish their new stamps to be instantly identified and appreciated.

CHAPTER NINE

ALL KINDS OF STAMPS

To say that stamps pay postage sounds simple enough, but it won't be long before the newcomer to stamp collecting realises that there are many different kinds of stamps within that definition, and it is best to be able to recognise them from the beginning.

The first and most apparent distinction is between definitives and commemoratives. Commemorative stamps are those issued for a special occasion, and usually for a limited period of time. Definitives are stamps intended for normal, everyday use, which are placed on sale at the post office for an indefinite period.

All the early stamps were therefore definitives, and many years went by before anyone thought of issuing stamps to mark a particular event or anniversary. The question of which stamps qualify as the world's first commemoratives has been the subject of much debate, but the honour is frequently accorded to a 5c. stamp issued by Peru in April 1871, on the occasion of the opening of the railway linking Lima, the capital, with Callao and Chorrillos. The design shows an early steam engine and the names of the three places concerned.

The so-called 'Laureated' issues of France, showing the head of Napoleon III crowned with a laurel wreath, which appeared in 1862, have been claimed as the first commemoratives since the laurel wreath celebrated the Emperor's victories in Italy, but they were really definitive in purpose. They lasted until 1870, and would doubtless have lasted longer still, had not the Franco-Prussian war intervened and brought the Emperor's reign to an abrupt end.

77

Stamps issued by New South Wales in 1888, on the centenary of the first British settlement in Australia, may be regarded as the first commemoratives of the British Commonwealth. This claim might be disputed on the ground that the series was in use for about eleven years, but on the other hand each design included the words 'One Hundred Years', the first commemorative inscription ever to appear on the stamps. Hong Kong was not far behind with a stamp of 1891 for the golden jubilee of the colony, but this was only an overprint on the regular issue.

The 1887 stamps of Great Britain are often referred to as the Jubilee issue, because their appearance coincided with the golden jubilee of Queen Victoria, but these were not commemoratives in the usual sense because they remained current until the reign of King Edward VII. Britain's conservative stamp-issuing policy meant that we had to wait until the British Empire Exhibition stamps of 1924–25 for the first real commemoratives.

The United States set the pattern for future commemorative issues with long sets for the Columbian Exhibition of 1893 and the Trans-Mississippi Exhibition of 1898: larger size than the normal stamps, interesting pictorial designs, often of an historical nature, limited printing and short period of currency. Between these two came the Belgian issue of 1896 for the Brussels Exhibition and a Greek set which I will mention later on.

By the early years of the twentieth century the idea of commemorative stamps was rapidly catching on elsewhere. In 1906 Barbados produced a set of stamps (a year late!) to mark the centenary of the death of Admiral Lord Nelson. In 1908 Austria issued a long series for the sixtieth anniversary of the accession of Emperor Franz Josef, and in the following year even China issued three stamps to celebrate the first year of a new Emperor's reign: two issues of much interest because only a few years later both monarchies were no more.

But the scatter of pre-World War I commemoratives was nothing to what came after. By the 1930s commemoratives were appearing thick and fast. From an early date exhibitions were a favourite subject for special stamps, and in 1931, on the occasion of the International Colonial Exhibition in Paris, came the first of the 'omnibus' issues, that is to say, stamps of similar character or design issued more or less simultaneously by a number of different countries to celebrate the same event. The pioneer omnibus of 1931 was shared by France and twenty-five of the French colonies – a set of four stamps from each. The first British Commonwealth omnibus followed with an even larger series in 1935 for the silver jubilee of King George V.

There have been a number of omnibus issues since then, but with one or two exceptions (such as the Coronation series of Queen Elizabeth II in 1953) they have not been very popular with collectors and it seems doubtful whether we will see many of them in the future.

Closely related to commemoratives in the philatelic family are the charity stamps – known in the United States, aptly enough, as semi-postals. These are the stamps, often commemorative in their nature, which are issued to raise funds for a good cause as well as to pay postage. They are sold by the post office like other stamps, but at a price above their postal value, the balance going to the charity concerned. The amount of this charity surcharge is usually given on the stamp in addition to the postal value, but not always.

Certain European countries have been most prolific with charity stamps: Belgium has issued just about as many stamps with a charity surcharge as without! In the British Commonwealth group they are much less frequent, perhaps the best known being the New Zealand Health stamps (with a premium in aid of children's health camps) which have appeared annually since 1929.

An early example of stamps issued mainly for other than

postal purposes is provided by Greece, which in 1896 issued a set of twelve stamps for the first Olympic Games of the modern era. This included stamps of a higher face value than Greece had ever issued before, and it was hoped that the proceeds of the sale of these to collectors would cover the administrative expenses of the games! The stamps were most unpopular at the time, and to a large extent they were boycotted. After four years remaining stocks were over-printed with lower values (a rare case of stamp 'devaluation') and used up as ordinary postage stamps.

In the latter form these Greek stamps were a somewhat unusual example of another philatelic category: the pro-visionals. These are stopgap issues brought out, often at short notice, to fill a postal or political purpose until such time as a permanent issue can be prepared. Most provision-als are caused by a sudden shortage of stamps of a particular value, often following a change in postal rates.

Others are of a different character. When the Gold Coast achieved independence as Ghana, for example, the existing stamps were overprinted 'Ghana Independence 6th March 1957' as a temporary measure. It was not until 1959 that Ghana's first definitive series appeared, although there were a number of very colourful commemorative sets in the interim.

A somewhat similar situation arose in Nyasaland, which became independent on the break-up of the Central African Federation in 1963. National pride demanded that inde-pendence should be recognised on postage stamps without delay, but the only stamps in existence bearing the name of Nyasaland were revenue stamps. So a 'Postage' overprint was applied which also crossed through the word 'Revenue' with two black lines, and the whole set pressed into postal service pending the preparation of a definitive issue.

As well as being provisionals of great interest, those Nyasaland stamps are perhaps the outstanding example of what are known in philately as postal-fiscals: stamps origin-

1852–57. *Imperf.*

A. *Thin wove paper.*

6	1	3d. red	£110	35·00
		a. Bisected, on cover ..		
7	,,	3d. deep red	£110	35·00
7a	,,	3d. scarlet-vermilion ..	£120	40·00
		b. Major re-entry	—	85·00
8	2	6d. slate-violet	£1300	£225
9	,,	6d. greenish grey	£1300	£225
9a	3	12d. black	—	£6500

B. *Medium hard wove paper.*

10	1	3d. red	60·00	25·00
11	,,	3d. deep red	60·00	25·00
11a	,,	3d. brown-red	75·00	30·00
		b. Major re-entry	—	65·00
		c. Bisected (1½d.), on cover	—	
12	2	6d. slate-violet	£1100	90·00
		a. Bisected (3d.), on cover ..	—	£1200
13	,,	6d. greenish grey	£1100	£100
14	,,	6d. brownish grey ..	£1100	95·00
14a	3	12d. black	—	£6500

C. *Thick hard wove paper.*

15	1	3d. red	£160	60·00
		a. Bisected, on cover ..	—	£1400
16	2	6d. grey-lilac	£1900	£250

D. *Very thick soft wove paper.*

17	2	6d. purple (reddish) ..	£950	£250
		a. Bisected (3d.), on cover ..	—	£1400

1857. E. *Thin soft ribbed paper.*

18	1	3d. red	£160	55·00

F. *Thin brittle wove paper.*

19	1	3d. red	£180	85·00

4. Jacques Cartier.

1855 (Jan.). *Imperf.*

A. *Thin wove paper.*

20	4	10d. bright blue	£600	£100
20a	,,	10d. dull blue	£600	£100
		aa. Major re-entry*	—	£180

B. *Medium wove paper, semi-transparent.*

20b	4	10d. bright blue	£650	£100
20c	,,	10d. Prussian blue	£700	85·00
		d. Major re-entry*	—	£180

1857. C. *Stout hard wove paper.*

21	4	10d. blue	£750	£100
		a. Major re-entry*	—	£180

These stamps may be divided into "wide" and "narrow," due to the shrinkage of the paper, which was wetted before printing, and which contracted unevenly when drying. The width varies from 17 mm. to 18 mm., the narrower being the commoner.

* The 10d. Major Re-entry listed shows strong doubling of top frame line and left-hand "8d. stg.", and line through lower parts of "ANAD" and "ENCE". There are other, lesser re-entries.

5

6

1857 (2 June). *Imperf.*

22	5	7½d. pale yellow-green ..	£700	£325
22a	,,	7½d. deep yellow-green ..	£750	£275

There are several re-entries in these stamps.

The same remarks apply to this stamp as to the 10d. blue. The width varies less, being generally 18 to 18½ mm.

1857 (1 Aug.). *Imperf.*

A. *Stout hard wove paper.*

23	6	½d. deep rose	75·00	30·00

B. *Thin soft ribbed paper.*

24	6	½d. deep rose (*horiz.*) ..	£300	£150
24a	,,	½d. deep rose (*vert.*) ..	£500	£250

1858–59. *P* 11¾. A. *Stout wove paper.*

25	6	½d. deep rose	70·00	50·00
25a	,,	½d. lilac-rose	85·00	50·00
26	1	3d. red	£110	35·00
27	2	6d. brownish grey	£650	£275
27a	,,	6d. slate-violet	£750	£225

B. *Thin ribbed paper.*

27b	6	½d. deep rose-red	—	£300
28	1	3d. red	—	£130

C. *Thick hard paper.*

28a	1	3d. red	—	£130

The 3d. is known perf. 14, and also *percé en scie* 13, both being unofficial, but used at the period of issue.

7

8. Beaver.

9. Prince Albert.

10

11. Jacques Cartier.

FOR WELL CENTRED COPIES ADD 100%
(Nos. 29/120)

(Recess. American Bank Note Co.)

(On 1st May, 1858, Messrs. Rawdon, Wright, Hatch, and Edson altered the name of their firm to "The American Bank Note Co.," and the "imprint" on sheets of the following stamps has the new title of the firm with "New York" added.)

1859 (1 July). *P* 12.

29	7	1 c. pale rose (to rose-red)	5·00	2·00
30	,,	1 c. dp. rose (to carm.-rose)	8·00	3·25
		a. Imperf. (pair)	£400	
		b. Imperf. × perf.		
		c. Laid paper	—	£1000
31	8	5 c. pale red	12·00	1·75
32	,,	5 c. deep red	12·00	1·75
		a. Re-entry*	—	55·00
		b. Imperf. (pair)	£400	
		c. Bisected (2½ c.), on cover	—	£300
33	9	10 c. black-brown	£400	90·00
		a. Bisected (5 c.), on cover ..	—	£650
33b	,,	10 c. deep red-purple ..	£275	60·00
		ba. Bisected (5 c.), on cover ..	—	£450
34	,,	10 c. purple (*shades*) ..	38·00	5·00
		a. Bisected (5 c.), on cover ..	—	£450
35	,,	10 c. brownish purple ..	38·00	6·00

D 41.	2 f. "Ochna"	..	..	5	5
D 42.	2 f. "Gloriosa"	..	..	5	5
D 43.	5 f. "Costus spectabilis"			5	5
D 44.	5 f. "Bougainvillea spectabilis"			5	5
D 45.	10 f. "Delonix regia"	..		5	5
D 46.	10 f. "Haemanthus"	..		5	5
D 47.	20 f. "Titanopsis"	..		8	8
D 48.	20 f. "Ophthalmophyllum"			8	8
D 49.	40 f. "Zingiberacee"	..		12	15
D 50.	40 f. "Amorphophalus"	..		12	15

The two designs in each value are arranged
se-tenant in "tete-beche" pairs throughout
the sheet.

MILITARY FRANK STAMP

M 1.

1963. No value indicated.

M 1.	M 1.	(-) lake	..	12	12

CANADA (N. AM.) (Br.)

A British dominion consisting of the former
province of Canada with Br. Columbia, New
Brunswick, Newfoundland Nova Scotia, and
Prince Edward Is.

1851. 12 pence = 1 shilling. (Canadian) =
1s. 3d. sterling.

1859. 100 cents = 1 dollar.

1.

2. Beaver.

3. Prince Albert.

4.

5. Jacques Cartier.

6.

1851. Imperf.

23.	1.	½d. rose	..	75·00	30·00
10.	2.	3d. red	..	60·00	25·00
2.	3.	6d. purple	..	£900	£140
22a.	4.	7½d. green	..	£750	£275
20.	5.	10d. blue	..	£600	£100
4.	6.	12d. black	..	£6000	£5000

1858. Perf.

23.	1.	½d. rose	..	75·00	30·00
26.	2.	3d. red	..	£110	35·00
27.	3.	6d. purple	..	£650	£275

		Values in cents.		Perf.	
1859.					
29.	1.	1 c. red	..	5·00	2·50
44.		2 c. red	..	25·00	12·00
31.	2.	5 c. red	..	12·00	1·75
37.	3.	10 c. violet	..	32·00	4·75
36.		10 c. brown	..	45·00	6·00
40.	4.	12½ c. green	..	30·00	3·50
42.	5.	17 c. blue	..	40·00	5·00

DOMINION OF CANADA

13.

14.

1868.

54.	13.	½ c. black	..	2·25	2·00
55.	14.	1 c. brown	..	25·00	2·25
76.		1 c. yellow	..	30·00	3·75
56.		2 c. green	..	30·00	2·50
58.		3 c. red	..	12·00	1·50
70.		5 c. olive	..	25·00	3·75
59.		6 c. brown	..	45·00	2·50
61.		12½ c. blue	..	25·00	2·50
113.		15 c. purple	..	3·75	2·00
67.		15 c. blue	..	10·00	2·50

16.

17.

1870.

101.	16.	½ c. black	..	20	15
80.	17.	1 c. yellow	..	75	5
82.		2 c. green	..	2·00	5
106.		3 c. red	..	75	5
107.		5 c. grey	..	1·40	5
88.		6 c. brown	..	3·75	75
118.	-	8 c. grey	..	3·50	25
112.	17.	10 c. magenta	..	4·00	1·25

On 8 c. head is to left.

18.

1893.

115.	19.	20 c. red	..	12·00	1·25
116.		50 c. blue	..	12·00	1·25

20.

21.

1897. Jubilee.

121.	20.	½ c. black	..	1·50	1·25
123.		1 c. orange	..	15	20
124.		2 c. green	..	30	35
126.		3 c. red	..	15	5
128.		5 c. blue	..	1·25	1·25
129.		6 c. brown	..	3·75	4·00
130.		8 c. violet	..	1·25	1·75

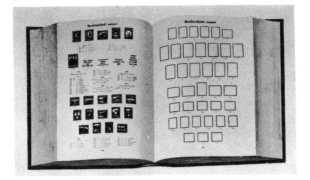

Two contrasting types of album. (a) The fast-bound printed album, with a catalogue on the left-hand page and opposite this, spaces for all stamps listed; (b) a typical spring-back loose leaf album offering scope for individual initiative in displaying stamps to good effect. This album has black leaves, but white leaves are more usual

How to use a modern, transparent perforation gauge. Move the stamp up or down until the points of the perforations match the converging lines – and read the number at the left. Readings to decimal points can be taken, if required, from the scale at the right

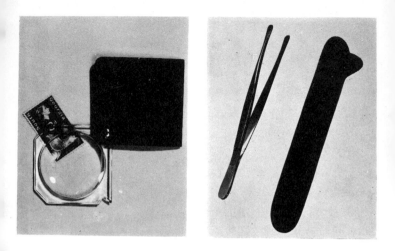

Some useful items for the collector's outfit: a pocket
magnifier, tweezers (with case), water-mark detector
tray, and colour guide

(a) Removing the leaves (in their inner cover) from a spring-back loose-leaf album. (b) Duplicate books are available in a wide variety of styles and sizes. They are a useful means of housing stamps until such time as they are mounted or otherwise disposed of. Whether in duplicate books or albums, transparent interleaving is a worth-while additional protection for stamps

The 'art' of the propaganda forgery! Apart from lacking perforations, this small sheet of four stamps appears on cursory glance to be the familiar 'Hitler Head' type of Germany, current during the Second World War. Closer examination shows that the design has been 'adapted' to give the head the appearance of a skull. In addition the normal inscriptions at the foot, DEUTSCHES REICH, has been altered to FUTSCHES REICH. The effect may be crude, but it was one of several parodies of German stamps, evidently the work of Allied propagandists, which appeared on the market at the close of the Second World War

Korea: The stamps that led to a Japanese invasion. Cook Islands: a ship at anchor with all sails set! British Honduras error of inscription. New Zealand: Lake Wakatipu wrongly spelt. Samoa: the hurricane stamp. Egypt: The Suez Canal issue

A Typical First-Day Cover. The 1964 Olympic Games issue of Cyprus, postmarked on the first day of issue. The stamps, like all modern Cyprus issues, are inscribed with the name of the country in three languages — Greek, Turkish and English

Art on stamps has become a popular subject for the thematic collector, especially in the last few years as the development of multicoloured photogravure for stamp printing has enabled designers to bring miniature versions of many famous paintings to the stamp album. Many works of art, however, are too large to reproduce effectively in stamp size. When St Lucia adapted William Hogarth's triptych from the Church of St Mary Redcliff at Bristol for the subject of its Easter stamps in 1970, the designer overcame the problem most ingeniously by spreading the painting over three stamps! All three were printed together in the same sheet to reproduce the painting in the correct proportions, but could of course be separated for normal postal use

An interesting commentary on the development of stamp design is given by these few examples of stamp centenary and other stamp-on-stamp commemorative issues

Odd shapes and sizes. Victoria (Australia) $\frac{1}{2}$d. of stamp of 1901 – one of the smallest ever issued; Denmark – the first stamps were square; a tall, thin design from Gibraltar and a long, narrow one from Botswana; a curious octagonal design from Thessaly, issued in 1898 and a five-sided Christmas stamp from Malta; an early triangular stamp of Newfoundland; and a self-adhesive 'free-form' novelty from Sierra Leone – in the shape of a map of that country

Examples of issues from eight countries which no longer have their own stamps: Saar and Heligoland (both now part of Germany); Danzig (later part of Germany, now part of Poland); Labuan (later part of Straits Settlements, now part of Malaysia); Zululand (later part of Natal, now part of South Africa); Georgia (now part of the Soviet Union); Crete (now part of Greece); and Queensland (now part of Australia)

Mauritius was the first British colony to issue stamps. The famous Post Office issue of 1847, consisting of 1d. and 2d. values is so called because the inscription at the sides reads 'Post Office' instead of the 'Post Paid' of subsequent issues. The design, engraved by a local jeweller, was obviously inspired by the Penny Black. This envelope, bearing two of the 1d. stamps in excellent condition, was discovered some seventy years ago in a sack of stamps on sale in an Indian bazaar. When it was sold in 1960, it fetched more than £158,000 – making it the most valuable envelope in the world. Including the two on the envelope, only fourteen of the 1d. value are known to exist, and only twelve of the 2d

GREAT BRITAIN 1841   CAPE OF GOOD HOPE 1861   BADEN 1851

U.S.A. 1918   CANADA 1959   INDIA 1854

Printed in Photogravure by Harrison & Sons Ltd.

Major printing errors have caused some of the greatest rarities known in philately. Six of them were reproduced on this souvenir of the 1960 London International Stamp Exhibition. The 1d. stamp of Great Britain with check letter missing from the lower right corner; the Cape of Good Hope 4d stamp, wrongly produced in the colour of the 1d.; a 9-kreutzer stamp from the German state of Baden, normally on rose-coloured paper, but printed in error on the green paper intended for the 6-kreutzer; and three spectacular inverted-centre errors from the United States, Canada and India

The idea of producing stamps in miniature sheets – consisting of as many as a dozen stamps or as few as only one – started on the Continent in the 1930's. Miniature sheets are intended mainly as souvenirs for collectors, although the stamps in them are of course equally valid for postage as those from normal-size sheets. The best-known British Commonwealth examples are the modern Health stamps of New Zealand. The elaborate form taken by some miniature sheets is illustrated by this example from the Maldive Islands ally intended for revenue or fiscal purposes but which, either by mistake or through an emergency of some kind, have received postal use. Stamp collecting is usually taken to mean the study of adhesive postage stamps only, and so postal fiscals, unless specifically overprinted for postage like the Nyasaland set, should preferably be collected on the original cover, proving that they have indeed passed through the post. Fiscal-postals, on the other hand, are simply stamps which are equally valid for postage or revenue purposes.

Then there are categories of stamps issued for particular postal services. Prominent among these are airmail stamps, which from non-English speaking countries can usually be identified easily enough by such words as Aereo, Avion, Flugpost, etc.

The carriage of mail by air goes back much further in time than many collectors realise. The first government-sponsored airmail flight took place in the United States in August 1859, when a balloon called the Jupiter carried mail from Lafayette to Crawfordsville, Indiana; the destination was intended to be New York, but contrary winds obliged the balloonist to descend. The centenary of this flight was marked by an American commemorative stamp.

The first service to be conducted over a period with some degree of regularity was arranged during the siege of Paris in 1870. The beleaguered city kept in touch with the rest of France by dispatching mail by balloon, inward mail being received by means of pigeons.

The first government-sponsored airmail flight by a powered aircraft took place between Allahabad and Naini in India, in February 1911, although there were experimental flights in France and Britain before this. The first such regular service was the 'Coronation Airmail' between London and Windsor in September of that year, when some 130,000 letters and postcards were carried, postmarked 'First United Kingdom Aerial Post'. The first international service, between Austria and the Ukraine, started in 1918, and in the following year regular airmail facilities were provided between London and Paris. Thereafter development was rapid.

In some cases mail has been carried by air without extra charge. The outstanding example was the Empire Air Mail Scheme, popularly known as the 'All-Up Service', introduced in 1937, by which all first-class mail between Britain and most of the major Commonwealth countries was normally carried by air. This service, however, was discontinued on the outbreak of the Second World War, and has never been resumed.

But airmail postage usually costs more than surface post, and over the years many stamps have been issued specifically or mainly for airmail use. Such stamps are known to collectors as airmails, air stamps, or simply airs. The earliest airmail stamp was inscribed 'Balloon Postage', issued in connection with a series of balloon flights in the United States in 1877. But the earliest government-issued airmail to be found in the standard catalogues was an overprinted issue of Italy in 1917 for an experimental service between Rome and Turin.

The balloon stamp just mentioned will serve to introduce another category of stamps, for this was a semi-official; that is, a stamp produced by a private firm or individual but with the agreement of the postal authorities. Probably the biggest and best-known group of semi-officials are the SCADTA issues of Colombia, which appeared in the 1920's and 1930's, and their successors. The initials stood for Sociedad Colombo-Alemana de Transportes Aereos (Colombian-German Air Transport Company), an airline which held the airmail contract and was authorised by the Colombian Government to collect airmail charges by means of its own stamps.

Any letter to be conveyed by airmail inside Colombia required the airline's stamp as well as the ordinary postage stamp, and this applied even to mail coming from abroad. The SCADTA issues were therefore placed on sale at Colombian consulates in various countries so that people wishing to correspond with Colombia by airmail could buy the necessary stamps and affix them to their letters. SCADTA stamps thus sold in other countries can be distinguished by large initial letters overprinted on them – another curious philatelic sideline.

The existence of such semi-officials should not confuse the beginner as to the meaning of the term 'official'. Strangely enough this does not usually mean a stamp officially issued by the authority of a national post office: this is taken for granted of any stamp, unless stated otherwise. Official stamps are those issued for the use of government departments only. Many countries have issued them in the past, and a few still do. India and Pakistan are notable examples, though here, to complicate the subject still further, they are known as Service stamps! British stamps were overprinted for use by several departments of the government from 1882 onwards, but the practice ceased after the reign of King Edward VII. An official version of the Penny Black itself (with the letters V.R. in the upper corners) was prepared for use in 1840 but never issued.

New Zealand issued official stamps for many years, but their use was discontinued in 1956, with one exception. The Life Insurance Department of the New Zealand Government retains the privilege, which it has enjoyed since 1891, of using its own distinctive stamps on its mail. Their designs, each featuring a lighthouse, are well-known to collectors.

Another type of stamp, which was sadly neglected by most collectors for many years but which is now claiming a greater share of attention, consists of the postage dues. These are stamps for postpayment of postage instead of prepayment. They are attached to mail by the Post Office to recover from the addressee charges due on items that are unstamped or understamped. They thus hark back to pre-stamp days when it was the usual practice for the recipient to pay the postage, not the sender.

France first issued postage due stamps as early as 1859, but Britain managed without them until 1914. The great majority of postage dues are strictly utilitarian affairs: a bold numeral to indicate the amount owing, an appropriate and brief inscription, and not much else. Generally the modern trend to large pictorial designs which has affected postage stamps has not yet spread to postage dues. But there are one or two exceptions. Back in 1924 Nyassa, a Portuguese territory in Africa (not to be confused with Nyasaland), brought out a series of triangular postage dues showing on various values African wild life as well as Vasco da Gama, the explorer, and his ship. In 1953 Monaco issued a postage due set depicting various forms of transport old and new, and these too were triangular in shape.

It has long been the practice to charge different rates for different classes of postal traffic, and this has led to numerous cases of special stamps for use on mail requiring special attention. Airmails, of course, are the most widespread example, but for a number of countries one can find express letter stamps and parcel post stamps. The United States had a stamp for Certified mail, and several nations have had distinctive issues for registered mail. Belgium has special stamps for use on railway parcels. Austria, back in 1851, was the first country to produce newspaper stamps. (Newspapers, of course, usually enjoy a concessionary rate of postage.)

A more curious example was Argentina's special issue in 1939 to pay the postage on gramophone records; the service was short-lived. Czechoslovakia has had special stamps for an additional fee which ensured delivery to the addressee in person. Stamps which appeared to show a somewhat pessimistic attitude were issued by the Netherlands in 1921; these paid the extra postage required on overseas letters to be placed in a special floating safe which would not sink in the event of a shipwreck! Known as marine insurance stamps, they are perhaps the oddest of the wide range of special-purpose issues.

Telegraph stamps, used on telegrams, are in contrast usually regarded as fiscals, and thus outside the scope of the majority of collections.

Finally, mention must be made of locals. Local stamps do not have general postal validity but are issued to prepay postage on some particular postal service or route, or in some particular locality. A few, in the early days, were issued by national post offices, but the great majority of locals have been 'private enterprise' stamps produced by organisations, companies or individuals providing postal facilities supplementary to (or in a few cases in direct competition with) the established postal systems.

Locals went out of favour when they were excluded from the general catalogues around the turn of the century, but in recent years there has been a revival of interest. Information about them must be sought in the more specialized publications; the earlier issues abound in forgeries and items of doubtful status, and used examples on cover are sometimes of exceptional rarity. So perhaps they are hardly a suitable field for the beginner. Nevertheless, if you come across a stamp which you suspect may be a local, put it by in your duplicate book until you find out something about it. One day it may introduce you to one of the most fascinating by-ways of the hobby.

Local stamps issued by the early city posts in the United States are keenly studied by specialists. The bygone locals of Russia and Sweden, among other places, have their followers. But not everyone realises that there are also a fair number of British locals. The stamps of the circular delivery companies, for example, are interesting. These companies were in business in the 1860s, undertaking to deliver circulars within a prescribed area for a farthing each. Since the lowest official rate of postage was still one penny, these facilities were welcomed by business men. Eventually the companies were suppressed on the grounds that they were infringing the postal monopoly of the state, but the public clamour was such that in 1870 a lower rate of postage was introduced for printed papers and with it, Britain's first half-penny stamp.

Locals of another kind are those produced on behalf of various offshore islands which don't have official postal facilities. These stamps are issued by the owners to pay the charges for carrying mail by their own transport as far as the nearest mainland post office. The extent to which some of them have received genuine postal use is doubtful, to say the least, but in at least two cases, Lundy and Herm, the local stamps have served a real postal need over a considerable number of years.

Lundy, the island in the approaches to the Bristol Channel, has had local stamps since 1929, and ranks as the veteran in this group. Herm, one of the smaller of the Channel Islands, issued stamps on mail carried by the island mailboat to and from Guernsey from 1949 until 1969, when the service was taken over by the Guernsey postal administration. But some of the so-called stamps for other tiny islands can hardly be regarded as more than publicity labels.

Somewhat comparable are the stamps issued by several hotels in isolated European health resorts in the period before the First World War, and again in the years between the wars. These were sold for conveying guests' letters to the nearest post office, and are now keenly sought after.

Whereas Belgium, as already mentioned, has its officially issued railway parcels stamps, in Britain the former independent railway companies used to issue their own stamps on 'railway letters' – packets which were conveyed by passenger train, to be called for or posted on arrival. Their modern descendants are the stamps produced for fundraising purposes by several of the famous narrow-gauge

86

railways operated with the aid of preservationist societies. Their postal necessity may be doubted, but they make interesting mementoes and the railway letter service for which they are issued does at least genuinely exist!

CHAPTER TEN

FORGED, FAKED OR GENUINE?

'Every stamp guaranteed genuine,' or some such phrase, is often seen on even the cheapest packets of stamps on sale in stationers' shops or department stores. Well, of course they are genuine! With so many common stamps readily available in large quantities, who would go to the trouble and expense of obtaining forgeries to put in cheap packets? It's a naïve claim, and although everyone knows that some stamps have indeed been forged (just as paintings and other works of art have been forged) the beginner should not be deceived into thinking that forgeries are lurking in every packet and stock-book. They are not.

Stamps are very difficult to forge. It is not easy (in fact it is practically impossible) to match the genuine stamp exactly in every tiny detail of design and lettering, in colour, in watermark and perforation, in the type of paper and the printing process. And of course the world's postal authorities, from the very earliest days of stamps, have taken care to put as many obstacles in the forger's way as possible!

Let it be emphasised straight away that in the case of beginners, spending modest sums on their stamps, the chance of being cheated by buying a forgery is so remote that it may be virtually ignored. This is simply because the forger can hope to secure a worth-while reward for his labours only by forging the more valuable stamps; cheaper stamps would just not be worth the effort.

There are three kinds of forgeries. First, and most interesting, are the postal forgeries: imitations of genuine stamps made to deceive the postal authorities, not collectors. These are the only examples of forgeries of common stamps, and they are usually a great deal more valuable to modern collectors than the genuine article! Postal forgeries on the original covers are of great rarity.

The early stamps of Spain were rather primitive in appearance, lacking the extremely fine engraving of Britain's first issues, and the authorities there were so worried by the possibility of large-scale forgery that for the first few years they changed the design every year, just to make the tricksters' task harder. The precaution was evidently justified, for as soon as they discontinued the practice, in 1857, forgeries became a serious problem.

Not all postal forgeries date back to the nineteenth century. A more recent example occurred in Australia in 1932, when the organisers of an illegal lottery printed their own stamps to send their literature through the post! At this time Australia issued special stamps for the opening of the Sydney harbour bridge, and the 2d. value of this set was forged, as well as the same value of the current definitive issue showing the head of King George V.

But the forgers made two mistakes. The watermark was missing and the perforations were wrong. Observant collectors quickly spotted something odd about the stamps, the authorities were alerted, and the criminals were apprehended and jailed.

In some countries it has long been the practice to allow stamps to be sold in tobacconists' and other shops as well as in post offices, and this provided the opening for another case of postal forgery in France in 1923. The stamp chosen was the widely used 25c. value in the well-known Sower design. Again it was philatelists who first noticed minor discrepancies and subsequently a couple were arrested with 25,000 forged stamps in their possession. Postal forgery or low-value stamps must clearly be carried out on the grand scale if it is to be financially worth while and of course the greater the number of forged stamps in circulation, the greater the risk of detection.

In Britain the only forgery of this type ever to cause serious concern was not so much a postal as a telegraphic forgery. This was a fraudulent imitation of the 1s. green of the 1867 issue, which was known and used only at the Stock Exchange post office in London. The forgeries were evidently smuggled into the building by a counter clerk who used them on telegram forms, pocketing the money he received for them. It was a simple and clever fraud because the stamps were never issued to the public in the ordinary way; the forms were kept by the Post Office for a stipulated period and were then destroyed.

The racket went merrily on and didn't come to light for some twenty-five years. Then a sack of forms which had accidentally escaped destruction was sold by a waste paper merchant to a stamp dealer. The stamp in question has letters in the corners, indicating its position on the sheet, and the dealer's suspicions were immediately aroused when he found certain combinations of letters which were not supposed to exist! An investigation was instituted, but doubtless due to the number of years which had elapsed, the guilty parties were never brought to trial.

Telegraph stamps, as I have mentioned, are usually regarded as fiscals, but the philatelic world makes an exception for the 'Stock Exchange forgery' as it is called, and high prices are paid on the infrequent occasions when one of them comes on the market.

In contrast to postal forgeries, philatelic forgeries are those made to defraud collectors. Such forgeries have been in existence for well over one hundred years, but many of the earlier ones are so crude that they are unlikely to deceive collectors even of limited experience. Undoubtedly it was those sturdy old nineteenth-century albums, with a space for every stamp, that caused the trouble in the first place. With growing numbers of collectors trying to fill all the spaces, it soon became apparent that there weren't enough of many of the early stamps to go around, and so the unscrupulous hastened to supply the need with forgeries.

Some of them, indeed, made no pretence of being genuine stamps, being printed in totally different colours. Productions of this kind, stamp-like labels plainly intended as space-fillers with no fraudulent intent, are known as facsimiles.

Britain, the United States and the continent of Europe have all had their share of notorious forgers. Their work has been studied and identified by specialists, and whole books have been written about some of them.

Probably the most dangerously skilful forger of all time was Jean de Sperati, who was born in Italy but lived in France. For more than forty years he produced imitations of rare stamps and got away with it by stating openly that they were facsimiles and never pretending that they were anything else. Unfortunately he supplied stamps to European dealers, and there was always the risk that these 'objets d'art' might find their way into dishonest hands.

Sperati was eventually obliged to give up his business owing to failing eyesight, but in 1953 the British Philatelic Association acquired his entire stock and all his records as a protection for future generations of philatelists. Most of his activities were restricted to European classics and a few South American stamps, and fortunately, perhaps, he did not turn his attention to many British Commonwealth issues. All Sperati's imitations are known and despite his immense skill and craftsmanship can be identified by experts from the printing process which he used; a combination of photography and lithography.

His method was to obtain a common genuine stamp, remove the design by chemical means so that he was left with completely authentic paper and perforations, and then superimpose on this his own impression of a much rarer stamp.

The third group, really a special kind of postal forgery, are the propaganda forgeries, made by one government to deceive another. They are wartime productions intended for the use of secret agents in the distribution of propaganda in enemy territory.

The Allied authorities towards the end of the First World War forged several of the low-value stamps of Germany, Austria and Bavaria – the latter at this date still had its own postal administration. But the extent of their actual postal use is doubtful. It appears that by the time they were ready the war was nearly over and they were no longer needed.

It was a different matter in the Second World War, when similar measures were adopted. A whole range of French stamps were forged in London and used by the resistance workers in occupied France. The forgeries not only deprived the enemy of postal revenue; they avoided the suspicion that might fall on Allied agents by the purchase of unusually large quantities of stamps at a post office. Another forgery was actually printed by the Maquis inside France in 1944.

The full story of these cloak-and-dagger stamps is never likely to be revealed, but it is known that a number of German stamps were also forged by both the British and the Americans.

Sometimes included in the category of propaganda forgeries (but better described in my view as propaganda labels) are the various crude imitations of British stamps produced by the Nazis, apparently in an attempt to undermine British prestige. They were so absurd that the effect must surely have been the opposite to what was intended!

There was a parody of the Silver Jubilee design of 1935, with the head of Stalin replacing the royal portrait and the inscription altered to read 'This war is a Jewish war'. The Nazis could not even get the spelling right: the word Jewish appearing as Jewsh. Another example aped the 1937 Coronation stamp, with Stalin's portrait substituted for the Queen's and the inscription referring to the Teheran conference: presumably with the implication that Britain was being dominated by Soviet Russia. A further 'phoney' imitated the current British 1d. stamp with the 'D' of the value in the form of a hammer and sickle!

Similar tricks were apparently played on the Allied side, for labels are known imitating German stamps but with Hitler's portrait replaced by a skull, and a suitably unflattering inscription.

Forgeries are not the only kind of spurious stamps. While a forgery may be defined as a fraudulent imitation of a genuine stamp, a fake is a genuine stamp which has been tampered with in some way to make it appear what it is not. False margins added to improve the appearance of a classic imperforate stamp; a postmark cleaned from the front and fresh gum added to the back to make a used stamp appear to be mint – these are examples of fakes. If someone trimmed off the perforations from a pane of stamps from a booklet and tried to pass it off as a rare imperforate variety, that too would be a fake.

It has been suggested that fakes are a greater danger to inexperienced collectors than forgeries, and that may well be true of those who wish to collect early issues. The high premium paid for classic stamps in extra fine condition is a great temptation to the faker; so is the growing interest in postal history, which has resulted in the appearance of quite genuine stamps on totally spurious covers, perhaps with a forgery of some rare postmark to complete the effect.

Then there are those items which are neither forgeries nor fakes but are bogus; in other words, they are complete impostors which have never existed at all in genuine form. Stamps have been produced, believe it or not, for countries which had no postal service at all, and even for countries which have never existed. One or two cases are known in which enterprising individuals have tried to increase their profits by adding a bogus value to a genuine set before selling it to collectors! Examples have been recorded of bogus postmarks, bogus overprints and even bogus perforations.

The authorities in Guatemala were most surprised to find what purported to be a Guatemala stamp being sold to collectors in 1867. It was totally bogus: Guatemala's first genuine stamps not appearing until 1871. In 1868 there was a similar case: a bogus Paraguayan stamp appearing two years before the first real ones. Then there was the remarkable hoax perpetrated by a Frenchman who announced that he had been elected King of Sedang, a remote area of Indo-China. He ordered his own stamps and sold some of them to collectors before his fraud was discovered.

Such schemes would stand little chance of success today; collectors are too knowledgeable and communications have improved. Nevertheless even since the last war there have been one or two instances of labels, issued by groups of eastern European exiles, being passed off as postage stamps. Some of the labels produced for the British offshore islands, already referred to, have been described as bogus, but in modern circumstances the distinction between a bogus stamp and a publicity label may not be easy to draw.

A recent example of an undoubtedly bogus issue occurred in 1962, when labels appeared purporting to be the stamps of a principality in Ireland called Thomond. Of course there is no such postal authority, and the labels, which appear to have been marketed mainly in the United States, were the subject of a successful prosecution by the Irish Post Office.

By this time I hope that the difference between a forgery, a fake and a bogus stamp has been made clear but there are a few items which do not seem to fall into any of these categories. For instance, in 1950 the South Moluccas, a group of islands in the East Indies, were reported to be the scene of an insurrection against Indonesian rule. The revolutionaries promptly had stamps printed in Europe, but the revolt collapsed and the stamps never had any genuine postal use.

Somewhat comparable in status are a curious German issue of the Second World War. At one stage in a remarkable fit of optimism, it seems the Nazis really believed they could march through the Middle East and invade and occupy India. Stamps were printed in Berlin in anticipation of this event, with the inscription 'Azad Hind' (Free India). But when it became clear that they would never be used for the intended purpose, they were sold to dealers in neutral countries.

Such stamps are not listed in the standard catalogues but they are interesting curios. Indeed, a collection of those stamps which come under the heading of 'prepared for use but not issued' would prove an absorbing study. By all means collect such things if they appeal to you, as long as you are quite clear what they are. In any case they would be better mounted in a separate album from the rest of the collection. What can only be deplored is any attempt to pass off such material to young collectors as genuine postage stamps.

After all this, it should now be reiterated that the average collector, and especially the beginner, has little to fear from forgeries, fakes and other suspect stamps. Remember that low-priced stamps are not worth forging, and in practice it is not unless and until you are in the market for stamps worth several pounds each that you need spare a thought for this darker side of the philatelic picture.

As in other collecting hobbies, the best safeguard is to buy such items only from well-established and reputable dealers. Such dealers make their living through selling to experienced philatelists, and they would not stay in business for long if their standards were suspect.

For really valuable stamps, or those in which any doubt persists, it is sound advice to obtain a certificate from one of the expert committees. In this country the Royal Philatelic

Society of London and the British Philatelic Association both have expert committees, and there are similar bodies in countries overseas, whose certificates are accepted all over the world. Each certificate is accompanied by a photograph. This is obviously essential, for without it there would be nothing to verify that the stamp in your possession is the one to which the certificate relates! It is common practice for auctioneers and dealers to offer rare stamps with a certificate as a guarantee of authenticity.

The expert committees have access to the knowledge and judgment of the leading authorities, and over the years they have built up valuable records and reference collections, which often enable them to pinpoint the work of individual forgers. Science has come to the aid of the hobby in this kind of detective work, and no matter how careful the forger may be his products can be detected by expert examination, coupled with the resources, where necessary, of the microscope, the ultra-violet lamp, and even X-ray photography.

A keen collector will soon begin to acquire the knowledge that will enable him to sort out at least the more obvious duds. With long experience he may even gain a sort of sixth-sense about forgeries. 'It doesn't look quite right to me,' he will say, casting a shrewd glance on a particular stamp and more often than not, he will be quite correct.

But common sense enters into the subject, too. If you are offered a stamp at what appears to be much less than the usual price, it may be a bargain – but it may also be a forgery. If you are offered a stamp in what seems to be unnaturally superb condition for the issue in question, suspect a fake!

Forgeries can add a certain spice to stamp collecting, but if you exercise reasonable prudence they need cause you no worry at all. Indeed, a beginner is quite likely to go on collecting happily for years without ever coming across a single one.

CHAPTER ELEVEN

STORIES BEHIND THE STAMPS

'All stamps are interesting, but some are more interesting than others.' I vividly recall an old-time collector telling me this – a man who had derived much pleasure from stamps for more than half a century and whose great delight was to share his knowledge and enthusiasm with others. 'And the most interesting of all,' he added, 'are the stamps that have a story to tell.'

For what are intended to be no more than miniature receipts for postage, stamps are amazingly complex things and some knowledge of the political, economic and social changes underlying a country's stamp issues can add immeasurably to the satisfaction of collecting.

Stamps not only reflect the march of world events: in some cases stamps have actually influenced them. Perhaps the best known example is the stamp design that decided the location of the Panama Canal.

The history of this canal is familiar enough: how De Lesseps, the famous French engineer who successfully built the Suez Canal, attempted the Panama project as well; how he was defeated by financial mismanagement and the fevers of the Central American swamps; and how later, with the advance of medical science, the canal was built by the Americans.

But if a group of American politicians had not changed their minds at the last moment, the canal would not have been built at Panama at all, but further north, through Nicaragua. A committee of the American Congress, in fact, reported in favour of the Nicaraguan route.

Just then Nicaragua brought out a new stamp issue, the design of which showed Mount Momotombo: a volcano in eruption. The pro-Panama group seized their opportunity; every supporter of the Nicaraguan route was sent one of the stamps, and with it a letter pointing out the risk to the canal from volcanic action if it were dug through Nicaragua. The result was that Congress decided on the Panama route and because of a stamp design Nicaragua lost the importance and prosperity which the canal would have brought.

The Panama Canal, incidentally, continues to have its impact on the stamp album. Ever since 1904 the Canal Zone has had its own stamps, the early issues being overprinted on stamps of the United States.

Let us now go back rather further in point of time, and across the Pacific to Korea. In the 1880's Korea was independent, though nominally under Chinese suzerainty. But the local nationalists were becoming increasingly alarmed by the growing Japanese influence over the government.

In 1884 the first Korean postal service was established. A new post office building was constructed by the Japanese in the capital city of Seoul, and a set of five stamps printed in Tokyo. In December of that year the Japanese held a banquet in the new building to celebrate the inauguration of the service, although only two of the stamps had by then arrived.

This was the last straw for the nationalists. In a bid for power, they seized the post office, symbol of hated Japanese influence, and scattered sheets of the new stamps through the streets. Then they burned the post office to the ground. For three days a murderous mob roamed the capital.

It was the very opportunity for which the Japanese had been waiting. On the ideal pretext of restoring law and order, troops moved in to occupy the country. It was the end of all hopes of Korean independence until 1945. And now modern Korean history is indicated by the separate stamp issues for the two zones into which the country has been divided since then.

The potentialities of stamps as a means of publicity and propaganda have been recognised for many years now. Stamps have been used to promote everything from achievements in outer space to export industries and tourist attractions. Such endeavours may be regarded as worthy enough, but on certain occasions stamps have also served to underline national aspirations in a more provocative way. One apparently innocuous issue even led to war in South America.

Bolivia and Paraguay had a long-standing dispute about a large border district, part of the cattle-ranching and agricultural area known as the Gran Chaco. It was claimed by both countries and in 1930 Bolivia issued its challenge, a stamp showing a map of the country with 'Chaco Boliviano' clearly marked. Not to be outdone, Paraguay replied in 1932 with a stamp showing a map of exactly the same area, but this time labelled 'Chaco Paraguayo'. In its inscription the stamp added a warning: 'Ha Sido, Es Y Sera.' (Has been, is and will be.')

The stamp war soon developed into real fighting, which went on intermittently for some years. The boundary was finally settled by arbitration in 1938, and in the following year Bolivia and Paraguay composed their differences at the Chaco peace conference in Buenos Aires.

Most of the disputed territory went to Paraguay, which then issued a stamp proudly displaying yet another (and larger) map of the Chaco, to commemorate an 'honourable peace'. What is more, feeling no doubt in a suitably generous mood, the Paraguayans added to the set another stamp showing the national flags of both contestants! One can hardly imagine the Allied powers paying a similar compliment to the Axis countries after the Second World War. Indeed there were protests as late as 1965 when

German aircraft with the swastika emblem were shown on British stamps marking the twenty-fifth anniversary of the Battle of Britain.

Another stamp expressing a political claim caused bloodshed in Arabia. After the First World War a certain Hussein Ibn Ali was set up with Allied support as King of the Hejaz. The Turks had abolished the ancient caliphate, but in 1924 Hussein issued stamps with an overprint announcing his proclamation as caliph, or leader of the Moslem world. This implied sovereignty over all the other Arab states, and as two of his sons were then rulers of Iraq and Transjordan, he was apparently in a strong position.

But Hussein reckoned without Ibn Saud, ruler of Nejd in central Arabia, who had ambitions of his own, and who was further provoked when Transjordan produced some stamps for a state visit by Hussein inscribed 'Commemorating the coming of His Majesty the King of the Arabs'.

Nejd could not retaliate on stamps, since it didn't have any. Instead, Ibn Saud resorted to arms. He invaded the Hejaz and soon forced Hussein into abdication and exile. Mecca, Hussein's capital, fell to the invaders only nine months after the offending stamps had first appeared. Before long the Hejaz was incorporated into Nejd, and so the modern state of Saudi Arabia was formed – all the direct result of the stamps that cost a king his crown.

Over the years some apparently strange subjects have been chosen for stamp designs, but there is usually a sound reason for them when you investigate. Of this group of stamp stories literally hundreds could be quoted, so just one recent example must suffice here.

A hurricane which hit Samoa in 1889 was one of the most severe ever recorded, and caused great damage – a surprising event, one might think, for commemorating with special stamps in 1970. Yet in other ways the hurricane was beneficial, for it literally 'dampened down' an international crisis. The 1880s were the period of German colonial expansion, and the Germans had ambitions of adding the native kingdom of Samoa to their empire. The Americans were prepared to resist this development by force of arms, and Britain, with other interests in the area, was also concerned.

All three powers sent warships to Samoa as tension increased, and when the hurricane struck there were three German vessels, three American and one British at Apia, the capital. By the time the storm abated, only one vessel of the seven was still in a seaworthy condition and that, ironically enough, was the sole British representative, H.M.S. *Calliope*.

In the face of natural disaster, national differences were forgotten. Many tales were told of heroic rescues, and the Samoans were instrumental in saving the lives of many of their would-be masters. The hurricane gave time for more peaceful counsels to prevail, and the eventual outcome was the Anglo-German-American agreement of 1899, under which the western islands of Samoa (the greater part of the group) became a German colony while the eastern islands were handed over to America. After the First World War, Western Samoa became a New Zealand dependency but since 1962 has again been fully independent. So the stamps in memory of the great hurricane were much more significant than might appear at first sight.

A smaller number of stamps can be found which passed almost unnoticed by collectors when they first appeared but which turned out to have unsuspected meaning later on. Such a stamp was the South African issue marking the first meeting of the Legislative Assembly of the Transkei. When it was released in December 1963 no one imagined that the event it celebrated would lead within less than three years to the assassination of the South African prime minister.

Dr Verwoerd, advocate of 'separate development' for the white and coloured races, was struck down as he sat in Parliament at Cape Town – murdered by a white man who was reported to have considered that the prime minister was doing too much for the black races and not enough for the white.

The stamp was a reminder that there is in South Africa another parliament where all the faces are black. This is the Legislative Assembly of the Transkei, and it sits in Umtata in the building depicted on the stamp. Larger than Switzerland in size, the Transkei is the first of the 'Bantustans', a state-within-a-state where 'one man, one vote' is the rule. It was one of Dr Verwoerd's greatest enthusiasms. So the stamp is a symbol of an interesting political experiment in addition to an assassination which hit the world's headlines.

Again, a stamp issued by Portuguese India, showing the arms of Prince Henry the Navigator, was interesting enough in itself, for it was Prince Henry whose planning inspired the discovery of the Cape route to India more than four hundred and fifty years ago. But when the stamp came out in June 1960, no one realised that it was to prove Portuguese India's last new issue.

These small settlements were among the oldest Portuguese possessions, dating from early in the sixteenth century, but when India became independent in 1947, Portugal showed no sign of relinquishing them. In the closing days of 1961, after some years of growing irritation in Delhi with these last vestiges of European power, Indian troops marched in on the orders of Pandit Nehru and the take-over was achieved against only token resistance.

A strangely ironic stamp was the Egyptian issue of July 1961 marking the fifth anniversary of the nationalisation of the Suez Canal, an event of 1956 that led to an international crisis of the first order and was followed by a short-lived Anglo-French occupation of the canal zone.

The maritime nations of the world had misgivings about what might happen to the canal management under Egyptian ownership. In the event, these fears proved unfounded. After its reopening in 1957, the canal was not only maintained in efficient working order, but was substantially improved.

So when the stamp appeared the Egyptians had something to celebrate, and the issue of the single large and very striking stamp was well justified. It depicted the bow of a modern vessel against a map of the canal. On the other hand if President Nasser had been prepared to wait another twelve years the canal would have become Egyptian property in any case in 1968, when the original concession expired.

By that time, however, the canal was closed again – with hostile Egyptian and Israeli forces lined up on either bank. Shipping routes have been diverted and after two major stoppages many shipping men doubt whether the canal will ever resume its former importance, even when the problems of the Middle East situation are finally resolved. The huge tankers now afloat are too large to navigate the canal, and are designed for the Cape route.

Crisis, achievement, war, disappointment and major changes in the pattern of world trade – all these can be thus detected in the design of a single stamp.

In an earlier chapter I have referred to some of the interesting circumstances in which overprints have been applied to stamps. Allied to these are surcharges. Some collectors say that they don't like such items, but if they ignore overprints and surcharges they miss some of the best stamp stories. Whenever the face value of a stamp is altered by overprinting, you may be sure there's a good reason.

On 20th December, 1956 Trinidad and Tobago issued a provisional stamp, the 2c. value overprinted with the new value of 1c. The date is significant: it was the time of the Christmas rush. The 1c. stamp covered the local rate for Christmas cards, and during that December was being used at the rate of about 100,000 a day. Stocks were running low but a fresh supply was on order from the printers in England. To be on the safe side, the postal authorities decided to have half a million 2c. stamps surcharged locally to meet a possible shortage.

As soon as the new shipment of stamps was ready, they were rushed out to Trinidad by air. But the aircraft bringing them was held up in London by fog and in New York by engine trouble. With the new supply expected hourly, existing stocks finally ran out on the morning of 20th December. The provisionals were reluctantly introduced at the G.P.O. in Port of Spain. That day nearly 82,000 of them were sold. The same night the new stock of regular stamps arrived safely and were duly put on sale the next day, leaving the provisional with an official life of only five and a half hours – one of the shortest on record.

In contrast to this philatelic cliff-hanger, Denmark has issued a good many surcharges over the years for no other reason than the sound economical one of wishing to use up stocks of certain values which through changes of postal rates were no longer required!

Nowadays great care and thought go into stamp design, and many countries have their stamp advisory committees consisting of leading collectors, artists and designers. In view of this the number of errors that have been perpetrated on stamps is positively astonishing! These form yet another group of stamps with a story, and it can be good fun hunting them. I am here referring to mistakes in the actual design, not to printing errors such as inverted centres, stamps printed in the wrong colours or with one colour missing, and so on, which are another interesting aspect of the hobby.

Fiji, for instance, has depicted a native canoe at sea with no one aboard, and Australia managed to put the wrong portrait on a stamp commemorating an explorer. Bearing in mind the complexities of British titles, one may perhaps forgive Greece for describing Sir Edward Codrington, the naval hero, as 'Sir Codrington' on one of the stamps commemorating the centenary of the Battle of Navarino in 1927; but one feels that Newfoundland should have known better than to promote Sir Francis Bacon to Lord Bacon on a stamp issued back in 1910. In 1928 Newfoundland slipped up again: on a map design the names of Cape Bauld and Cape Norman, on the Newfoundland coast, were inadvertently reversed. This was put right when the design was redrawn in the following year.

Maps, however, have proved a snare to stamp designers on several occasions. As recently as 1969 it appeared from close examination of two Guernsey stamps that the Channel Islands had suddenly been removed from the English Channel to the middle of Spain! What had happened was that the map shown on the stamps gave a Latitude of 40 degrees 30 minutes instead of 49 degrees 30 minutes North.

Even more remarkable is the fact that one or two countries have made spelling mistakes on their stamps. In 1898 New Zealand issued a stamp inscribed 'Lake Wakitipu' instead of 'Lake Wakatipu', and North Borneo, in 1950, even contrived to spell the name of its own capital wrongly: Jessleton instead of Jesselton.

An error of a different kind is exemplified on all four values of a set issued by British Honduras in 1966. They are inscribed 'Postal Centenary'. But a postal service existed in British Honduras long before 1866 – postmarks from the capital of Belize being known from as early as 1800. The stamps should have been inscribed 'Stamp Centenary'.

Just occasionally one can find more than one mistake on a single stamp. In 1956 Italy issued a stamp on the 50th anniversary of the opening of the Simplon tunnel beneath the Alps, which has given its name to one of the world's most famous trains, the Simplon-Orient express linking Paris and Istanbul. The stamp was intended to show the Italian end at the time of opening, contrasted with old-fashioned mailcoach transport.

But it would be hard to imagine a worse railway 'howler'. The stamp shows a steam-hauled train, whereas the line was electrified from the beginning; it shows twin tunnels, although there was only one to start with, the second being opened in 1921; and even if this had been correct, the stamp still shows the train running on the wrong track!

Another surprising mixture of errors occurs in a Cook Islands stamp of 1932, purporting to show the arrival of Captain James Cook in 1773. To start with his ship, the Resolution, is shown with all sails set, which obviously would not be the case if the vessel had just dropped anchor for a landing party to go ashore. Then the stamp shows Cook and his party being greeted by the natives, when on this occasion they found the island uninhabited.

In 1774 Cook discovered the island of Niue. Here he received such a hostile reception from the inhabitants that he named the place Savage Island. But this fact didn't prevent Niue from issuing a stamp of precisely similar design to the Cook Islands issue!

An entirely new complexion was placed on the familiar phrase 'wind of change' by a Ghana stamp of 1957. This depicted an old-time galleon with the sails blowing in one direction and the flags in another.

For many years St Kitts-Nevis persisted in issuing stamps which showed Columbus discovering the islands through a telescope which had not then been invented. But this was not really a stamp error. The designer simply copied the seal of the colony where the mistake originated.

In this chapter I have space to do no more than suggest the scope of one of the most fascinating aspects of stamp collecting, the study of the stories behind the stamps, and to give one or two examples of different kinds.

There are thousands of such stories if you look for them. If you think that must be an exaggeration, I may add that for more than a decade now I have been writing a weekly press article about stamp stories, and there is still no sign at all of any shortage of subjects!

While it is true, as my old friend said, that some stamps

are more interesting than others, please remember that almost every stamp has some kind of story to tell, and there is great pleasure and satisfaction in finding something of interest about a stamp that other collectors have overlooked.

CHAPTER TWELVE

THE LURE OF POSTMARKS

Postmarks have a much longer history than stamps, going back to the days of the Bishop Mark and Dockwra's London Penny Post in the seventeenth century. The beginner should be clear in his mind, however, regarding the difference between postmarks in general and cancellations.

Cancellations (some people prefer the word obliterations) are simply the type of postmark which cancels a stamp to prevent it from being used for postage a second time. Postmarks take in marking of many kinds applied to the mail by postal authorities, and their study in conjunction with stamps, and as forerunners to stamps, can be an absorbing pastime.

As we have seen the original purpose of postmarks was to indicate the time of posting, and this remains one of their most important functions. But they also include the place of posting, and in pre-stamp days many of the town postmarks incorporated the mileage from London as a means of facilitating the calculation of the postage to be collected from the addressee.

When the first stamps were issued in 1840, they were cancelled with a Maltese Cross device, the variations of which are keenly collected by specialists. A little later in Victorian times the place and time of posting and the cancellation were combined into a single postmark, the post town being indicated not only in plain language but by a code number incorporated in the obliteration. This kind of marking, known to collectors as a duplex, was introduced in 1844 and lasted into the early years of the twentieth century.

As the quantity of mail increased, machine cancellations

were introduced and the early experimental versions of these are much sought after.

Postmarks have been collected in Britain and in the United States for about a century, but it is only in the last thirty or forty years that they have become really popular. It is worth a beginner's while to look out for interesting postmarks because although a number of societies have now been formed to cater for postmark collectors it remains true that postmarks are still not so widely collected, and have not been studied for so long or in such detail, as stamps. So you are more likely to pick up a scarce postmark as a bargain than a scarce stamp!

No doubt postmarks first began to exercise their appeal when stamp collectors realised that an unusual postmark could add greatly to the interest and value of a quite ordinary stamp. French stamps were used by Napoleon III's troops in Italy before that country was unified in 1870. Resulting from another war, Argentine stamps were used in Paraguay before the latter country had any stamps of its own. And the only way such interesting postal usage can be detected is by study of the postmarks.

Ever since the end of the eighteenth century wars of one kind and another have been the cause of many special postmarks. Enthusiasts can be found who collect anything from the markings used on letters sent home by prisoners in the Anglo-Boer War to the numerous Field Post Office postmarks which indicate the progress of the Second World War. All sorts of postmarks can be found, if you are lucky, from military campaigns of the past.

International postage has always been of great interest to collectors, and much research has been carried out into the postmarks applied to overseas mail in the pre-stamp era. There were two main types: ship letters, which were carried by private ship, and packet letters, conveyed by a vessel either maintained by the government or operating under a Post Office contract.

Many ports in the U.K. and in the British colonies overseas began using ship letter postmarks in the 1760s. But with the introduction of steamships their numbers began to decline, though a few were still in use in the early 1900s. India letters were a comparatively short-lived variant of ship letters brought in by the ships of the East India Company who had a special arrangement with the Post Office. Separate postmarks were required for these because the postage rates were different, and they lasted only from 1815 until steamers took over in the 1840's.

Packet letter postmarks, on the other hand, came in during the 1840's and were used for some sixty years. Postage on packet letters was higher than on ship letters because of the greater frequency and reliability of the service.

Paquebot (not to be confused with a packet letter) is a French term used internationally since 1894 on postmarks applied to mail posted on board ship. Shipboard mail is another popular sideline and an interesting collection can be formed of covers carried by famous liners.

Mail was first carried by rail on the pioneer Liverpool and Manchester Railway within less than a year of its opening in 1830. For mail transport the new railways quickly proved a great advance on the old mailcoaches and from this sprang the idea of speeding up the mails still further by sorting them actually on the train. A 'travelling post office', as it was called, was introduced in 1838 between Birmingham and Liverpool, and proved to be the first of many, similar arrangements being adopted in most of the major countries all over the world. The name is retained to this day, though usually abbreviated to the initials T.P.O., and the mail sorted and cancelled in a travelling post office usually bears an identifying postmark. More material for the post mark collector is provided by the mobile post offices. These are installed not in trains but in motor vehicles, and in many countries travel round from place to place providing postal facilities on special occasions, such as agricultural shows, big sporting events and the like.

Slogan cancellations – a convenient and inexpensive means of putting over a simple message to the public – were first introduced at the time of the First World War, and over the years have been used for imparting the government's advice on everything from investing in National Savings to making sure that your name is on the voter's list.

There was no British stamp for the wedding of Princess Elizabeth (the present Queen) but there was a slogan-type postmark incorporating wedding bells and this found its way into many collections.

In recent years the British Post Office has relaxed its former conservative policy and has allowed local authorities the use of slogan postmarks. With these local events have been publicised, seaside resorts have extolled their attractions, and development areas have earnestly invited new industries.

Yet another type of world-wide collection which can provide plenty of interest and amusement is the amassing of strange and unusual place-names in postmarks. One can understand that certain communities are pleased to be known by such names as Heart's Delight, Paradise and Success. But one certainly wonders how others came to acquire the less attractive names of Badlot, Peculiar, and even Ugley! If you wish to obtain a postmark from Hell you may do so for there is a village of that name in Norway. Or if you prefer an Odd postmark you can have that too, for the United States has a place (and a postmark) called Odd, and in Denmark there is an Odder! Australia, incidentally, is a happy hunting ground for interesting postmark place-names of Aboriginal meaning.

Any chapter about postmarks would be unthinkable without some reference to the cult of 'used abroad', that is, stamps which by their postmarks can be shown to have been used in some country other than the country of origin. It is a bigger subject than one might suppose.

Perhaps the classic example is Hong Kong, whose stamps in days gone by were used in the Chinese treaty ports and in Japan. But at various times in the last century British stamps were used not only in Gibraltar, Malta and Cyprus but also at many points in the West Indies, in Central and South America and in Morocco and the Middle East, where British postal agencies existed, and they were also used in Egypt by the British forces stationed there.

A few of these agencies lasted until quite recent times. The British post offices in Morocco and at Tangier for many years had British stamps specially overprinted, and in the Persian Gulf British stamps surcharged with new values in the local currency remained in use until 1966.

French stamps, too, were at one time quite widely used abroad, and the Italians, Russians, Austrians and Germans have all operated overseas post offices, with distinctive postmarks at various periods, notably in the Middle East, or Levant as it is better known to philatelists.

There are even some stamps which are cancelled before they are ever used in the post! These are called pre-cancels, and are particularly well-known among the issues of the United States, France and Belgium. Such stamps are bought by large organisations for the posting of mail in bulk, and to save time in dealing with such items the postal authorities cancel the stamps with a special postmark before selling them to the customer.

The modern craze for first-day covers – envelopes bearing a set of stamps postmarked on the first day of issue – is connected with postmarks, for postal administrations in many countries provide special first-day cancellations and recently even Britain has jumped on the band wagon.

Some of the modern covers specially printed for this purpose are extremely attractive, but somehow they don't seem as interesting to me as the old-time covers, posted without collectors in mind, where the postmarks may provide useful evidence of the date and circumstances in which a particular stamp has been used.

How do you collect postmarks? If there is enough of the postmark on the stamp to be legible, that makes it a perfectly collectable item, but of course it is better to have the complete postmark, and that means that it is better collected 'on piece,' that is a piece of the original cover, trimmed where possible to a neat rectangle, large enough to show all the postal markings as well as the stamp. If you are fortunate enough to obtain anything really unusual, a rare or early item, on a complete cover, then it should certainly be left that way.

In this chapter it has been possible to do no more than suggest a few of the ways in which postmarks can widen the scope and interest of the hobby. So remember: whenever you examine a used stamp, always take a good look at the postmark too!

CHAPTER THIRTEEN

COLLECTING TO A THEME

Through sheer weight of numbers it is becoming more and more impracticable to collect the stamps of the whole world, and so collectors have in recent years started looking for new ways of collecting. The most important of these is thematic collecting which has grown to great popularity over the past twenty years or so.

Thematic collecting means disregarding the geographic and historical aspects and arranging stamps according to the subject of the design rather than the country and date of issue.

Thus one may collect railways on stamps, ships, aircraft or motor-cars on stamps, heavy industries or native handicrafts, trees, birds or even insects on stamps, and so on.

Thematic collecting adds a new dimension to other existing interests. Zoologists may find great interest in a collection of rare animals on stamps, just as architects may appreciate stamps which show the finer points of famous buildings. Doctors and nurses may collect those issues with subjects related to medicine.

If you have a liking for music, you may like to study the many stamps that show distinguished musicians and composers, musical instruments, opera houses and the like. Children and education on stamps would make a good theme for a schoolteacher. Stamps with religious motifs offer a wide field, of which Christmas issues are just a part. Almost every kind of sport you can name has been featured on stamps somewhere or other, and maps on stamps are another interesting subject. A few stamps can even be found with a bearing on the topics of strong drink and temperance! And if you are a keen gardener you can develop a new kind of garden in your stamp album where the flowers will always be in bloom and where pests are unknown.

All these are fairly obvious topics for the thematic collector – thematics, incidentally, are known as 'topicals' in the United States – and it must be confessed that over the past decade especially a considerable number of stamps have appeared that seem expressly intended to find a home in the thematic collector's albums!

But there are other thematic subjects which can be geared to conventional stamp collecting. For example, stamps which depict the development of flight, from the mythical exploits of Icarus to the era of balloons and airships and on to the giant airliners of our own day, would form an interesting corollary to a collection of airmail stamps as such, though of course there are many items which would equally qualify for both.

Leading on from this is the story of space flight, and this has proved one of the most popular of all stamp themes. A worthwhile collection can be built up showing space achievements from the first Soviet sputnik right up to America's momentous landing of the first men on the surface of the moon in 1969, with doubtless many more issues to be added in the years ahead.

Again, a subject of keen interest to most collectors is the development of the postal service in many parts of the world, and this too is a story which can be told through stamp designs. Postal reformers, post office buildings, mail-coaches and mail vans – all these can be portrayed in the album, and so can the worthy postmen on whom the whole system depends.

Even stamps are depicted on stamps! In 1940, despite the exigencies of wartime, Britain issued a set of stamps to mark the centenary of the Penny Black. Unlike Mexico's issue on the same occasion, they did not actually reproduce the entire design of 1840. For that, collectors of British stamps had to wait for the 'Philympia' issue of 1970. But they did include the head of Queen Victoria that appeared on the first stamps. Long before this, Denmark brought out an interesting set of three small-sized stamps in 1926 on the seventy-fifth anniversary of the first Danish issue, adapting the designs of 1851 which had in fact been square, not rectangular. These commemoratives were strongly attacked at the time as a completely unnecessary issue, aimed only at collectors' pockets. But what the critics would have said if they had foreseen the present situation I hate to think!

Over the past twenty years or so many countries have reached their stamp centenaries and few have refrained from reminding us of the fact with a set of commemoratives. Soon, no doubt, the first of the one hundred and twenty-fifth anniversaries will be in the pipeline! First in the field with the idea of producing on a new stamp a facsimile of its own stamp in use one hundred years previously was Mauritius, whose stamp centenary set appeared (six months late!) in 1948. And since then the stamps-on-stamps theme has never looked back.

So keenly have collectors acquired such issues that one or two countries have joined in without waiting for the formality of a stamp centenary. Thus the Maldive Islands, in the Indian Ocean, celebrated the fifty-fifth anniversary of their first issue with a handsome set of stamps-on-stamps which came out in 1961.

Guyana, the former British Guiana, didn't bother to refer to an anniversary at all when producing a couple of stamps in 1967 which reproduce the famous 1c. British Guiana stamp of 1856. The original of this sold for a staggering 280,000 dollars (about £116,000) at a New York auction in March 1970 – far and away the highest price ever paid for a single stamp.

It is often called the world's rarest stamp, and Guyana thus described it when the facsimiles appeared in 1967.

This claim, however, is not strictly true. It is certainly the world's most valuable stamp, and there is none rarer, since only one example is known. But several other great rarities share this distinction and are thus equally rare. On the other hand, 'The world's equal-rarest stamp' would make an odd inscription and whether this stamp-on-stamp design may be regarded as another item for our list of designer's errors must remain a matter of opinion!

From this the reason for the appeal of stamp-on-stamp issues is plain to see. Many of the earlier issues of the nineteenth century are now so rare and expensive as to be beyond the reach of the average collector. The stamp centenary and similar issues do at least provide him with the chance of adding facsimiles of these famous stamps to his collection at a tiny fraction of the cost of the originals, yet without having to mount anything which is not a genuine stamp.

Even more interesting, sometimes, can be the less frequented thematic paths. For example, how about the history of exploration? This is such a large subject that it could be divided into several sections: the finding of the New World; the discovery of the Cape route to India; in a later age the epic voyages of Captain James Cook; and in modern times the story of Antarctic exploration.

As regards buying stamps the thematic collector can experience both advantages and disadvantages. On the credit side, your interest may be in a stamp design because it happens to show, for example, a railway bridge. But you don't need all the stamps in that design, and you certainly are under no necessity to obtain the highest and most expensive value; an inexpensive, lower value will serve your purpose just as well. On the other hand a dealer may be somewhat loth to break up a long set and sell you a single stamp out of it just because that one (but none of the others) chances to depict a particular flower! Against this the thematic collector does not have to concern himself with completing sets or with hunting some elusive perforation variety as other collectors do.

Thematics are also an essentially individual way of collecting; no two thematic collections will be alike, let alone identical, and it is entirely up to the collector's initiative and inclination just how wide or how narrow the scope of his chosen theme.

Ships on stamps, to quote a popular instance, would be a large subject indeed, ranging from small native canoes to sailing yachts, galleons, modern warships, passenger liners and the rest. To choose passenger liners alone would be a much smaller sea in which to fish, and North Atlantic passenger liners rather smaller still, though still big enough to be interesting. In passing, a collection devoted to the pirates and privateers of the Spanish Main would be attractive – and quite a few of the West Indies have issued stamps with a bearing on the subject.

One theme can lead to another. The ships-on-stamps enthusiast collecting designs which feature oil tankers might find himself starting another collection devoted to the oil industry!

It is only fair to warn beginners that some collectors tend to look down their noses on thematics as not being 'real stamp collecting'. Their numbers are becoming steadily fewer. So beginners should also be warned, if their preference is for thematics, to take no notice at all of the critics! Stamp collecting, after all, is a hobby wherein every collector is free to please himself; and it is surprising how many apparently highbrow collectors are coming round to the idea that thematics are a worth-while aspect of the hobby, sometimes even to the extent of adding a few thematic pages to their own collections.

As regards presentation, a thematic collection obviously involves different problems from a conventional collection. For one thing it is hard to imagine how a thematic display could be arranged in anything other than plain, loose-leaf albums.

Just as a conventional collection is usually arranged according to country and date of issue, so a thematic collection is seen to better advantage if the stamps devoted to different sections of the subject are grouped together. A collection of animals on stamps might begin with a few pages of prehistoric and mythical creatures, followed perhaps by a page of elephants, a page of giraffes and so on, until all the wild animals were covered. Next would come farm animals, and then domestic pets.

A greater quantity of writing-up is acceptable in a thematic collection, and such items as photographs, drawings, maps and so on can be used if desired to illuminate the theme. But there is a danger here: the ancillary material may loom so large that it tends to overshadow the actual stamps. I have seen a few thematic collections, beautifully written-up, in which the stamps seem to have been added almost as an afterthought! So let's not forget that even in thematics we are concerned, first and foremost, with a collection of stamps. As far as possible, let the stamps tell the story.

It is a tribute to the ingenuity of stamp designers that there is hardly a single aspect of life, work and leisure that cannot be illustrated by stamps. Collecting to a theme can be very satisfying and great fun, particularly if you can think of an unusual theme or treat a common one in an unusual way. Why not try it and see?

CHAPTER FOURTEEN

ORGANISED PHILATELY

In a hobby of essentially please-yourself appeal, it may seem strange at first to think of stamp collectors being *organised*. But collectors are usually gregarious folk who realise the advantages of associating with others of similar tastes.

This may be achieved simply by a few friends meeting in their own homes to compare their collections. But on a somewhat larger, but still friendly scale there is now hardly a town of any size in this country without its own stamp club or philatelic society.

Occasionally one hears of people who find the latter term a little off-putting; who believe that such societies are only for learned and experienced philatelists and that beginners would feel out of place in such erudite company. Nothing could be farther from the truth. Local societies welcome beginners, who will find that the subscription of perhaps £1 a year is an excellent investment.

A few of our leading provincial societies are seventy years old or more; a number of others were successfully established in the 1930s. But the great growth of the philatelic-society movement dates from the immediate post-war years when the hobby experienced a boom which has been continuing ever since.

A small society may have perhaps fifty members; a larger one may have several hundreds. Many have flourishing junior sections, frequently with a lower age limit of fourteen, giving young collectors most of the advantages of adult membership for a very modest subscription.

Meetings are held probably once or twice a month for most of the year at some convenient centre. They are friendly, informal affairs where the amount of 'business' is kept to a minimum to allow plenty of time for the main attraction. This may be a talk and display from a visiting speaker. (I never cease to be impressed with the tremendous amount of time and effort which some of our most prominent philatelists devote to thus supporting local societies up and down the country.) Or it may be a quiz, an auction, a brains trust, a competition or a film or slide show.

To discover and encourage the budding speakers of the future, there are usually occasional meetings with such titles as 'My Favourite Album Page and Why', or 'Five Sheets – Five minutes' when members are asked to show some of the stamps that appeal to them most and to talk about them for a few minutes.

The customary procedure is for the speaker to have his say and then exhibit his material on the display boards. Then the members have an opportunity to examine them. (In the smallest societies the exhibits may be passed round from hand to hand, being protected by transparent plastic covers.) After that there is time for questions and discussion, which can often prove the most interesting part of the evening!

One thing you may be sure of: plenty of opportunity will be provided for the members to get together to buy, sell, exchange and discuss stamps among themselves.

Then visits will probably be exchanged with neighbouring societies. From these have grown a number of county federations of philatelic societies which do good work in promoting the hobby by arranging local exhibitions and so forth. In addition a lively society will arrange outings to important national exhibitions and other events and places of philatelic interest.

All this is not the end of the usefulness of the local society. There will probably be a library of philatelic books and catalogues which for a copper or two, or very likely without any charge at all, may be borrowed at one meeting and returned at the next. The library is a valuable source of information, and wise beginners will make full use of it. As mentioned in Chapter 3, the majority of societies also run a circulating exchange packet, and this as previously explained can be a splendid means of increasing both your collection and your knowledge.

With growing specialization and limitation of collections, it may be wondered whether local societies catering for all kinds of collectors within a particular town or locality may have a less important role in future. Well, there's certainly no sign of this happening as yet! The true enthusiast never tires of looking at stamps, any sort of stamps, whether his own or other people's. And although the specialist in the issues of the Australian States may appear to have little in common with the man who collects British postmarks or the modern stamps of the United States, the lure of philately in general brings them together to compare notes and examine one another's collections at the meetings of their local society.

For one thing, each one may be hoping in the back of his mind to convert the others to his particular interest! For another, they are all united in their wish to support the society's activities and to help the less experienced members in every way they can.

Perhaps the secret of the local society's success is that the members have learned that they can get more out of their hobby by sharing it with others than by keeping it to themselves.

Most of the societies are affiliated to the British Philatelic Association which also has both collectors and dealers as individual members. Another leading organisation is the National Philatelic Society, with members all over the country and overseas, which has a noted reference library and holds meetings in London. The N.P.S. was formerly known as the Junior Philatelic Society, its title alluding not to the age of its members but to the fact that it was founded after the august Royal Philatelic Society.

The local societies also send delegates to the Philatelic Congress of Great Britain. This, too, has individual members as well as affiliated societies. Congress holds an annual four-day gathering, a veritable parliament of British philately, at which papers are presented and debated, and resolutions discussed. It is at these Congress meetings that the famous Roll of Distinguished Philatelists is signed with due ceremony. This was inaugurated in 1921, and the first signature is that of King George V. To be invited to sign the Roll is perhaps the highest honour that any collector can achieve.

Congress also organises the Melville Awards, an annual competition for young collectors under twenty-one. The winning entries are exhibited at the Congress meetings, and the competition is named after Fred J. Melville, a famous figure in the history of philately, who founded the Junior Philatelic Society in 1899.

To cater for more specialized interests there has sprung up over the past twenty years a large and growing number of societies devoted to a particular group of stamps or a particular aspect of the hobby. Their membership is usually scattered rather thinly around the British Isles, and so most of their activities are conducted by post, although special functions such as exhibitions and conventions are held from time to time to give members the opportunity of meeting socially. Such societies circulate a newsletter or journal which may be of modest appearance but which in content is frequently of an extremely high standard, containing much information not available elsewhere.

For all the most likely groups and quite a few of the more unlikely ones, there are now active organisations of this nature, and as soon as your interests have crystallised sufficiently, it will be well worth your while to join the appropriate one.

The Canadian Philatelic Society of Great Britain and the Australian Commonwealth Specialists Society are two notable examples which come readily to mind but there are many others. Whether you collect South Africa or Spain, Egypt or Ethiopia, there is a specialist group, from whom you can learn a great deal, waiting to welcome and encourage you.

An interesting result of the increasing interest in postal history is the success of the Postal History Society. There is also the more exclusive Society of Postal Historians with a limited membership of experts which may be joined by invitation only. Such restrictions, however, are rare in philately.

A small group of collectors who meet or correspond to further their own particular interests are known as a study circle, and it is from these study circles that the larger specialized societies have grown. So if your interest runs to some out-of-the-way country whose stamps do not yet have a society devoted to them, the answer is clear: Start a study circle!

One further organisation deserves mention: the Philatelic Traders' Society. As its name implies, this is strictly for dealers only, and so it may appear to be of little interest to collectors. But in fact, although like any other trade association it exists to promote the interests of its members and to help them in their business activities, it also does much to support the hobby in general, in particular by organising STAMPEX, Britain's national stamp exhibition, held in London in March each year in conjunction with the National Philatelic Society.

P.T.S. members also subscribe to a professional code of conduct which is enforced by the Council of the Society, who have the ultimate sanction of explusion, which can be applied if necessary to any member who offends. So it is a useful safeguard for collectors to make sure of buying stamps only from dealers who are well-established P.T.S. members and whose integrity and reliability are beyond question.

Collectors, of course, can be as organised or as disorganised as they choose in pursuing their hobby, but organised philately succeeds to a remarkable degree in bringing together on an equal footing people of widely different backgrounds, occupations and ages.

Some years ago a well-known architect went on a tour of inspection of a large new house which he had designed and which was nearing completion. He was accompanied by several colleagues. While they were examining the building, along came a fitter to connect the gas meter. To the surprise of the onlookers, the architect and the fitter greeted each other as old friends, as indeed they were. For both were keen members of their local philatelic society.

By taking up stamp collecting you have access, if you wish, to a brotherhood which is not just local but national and even international in character, united in affection for the humble postage stamp.

CHAPTER FIFTEEN

'WHAT'S IT WORTH?'

An occupational hazard of stamp dealing is to receive the occasional visitor who produces from some deep recess of pocket or handbag a tattered example of some fairly old but extremely common stamp and asks the inevitable question: 'What's it worth?'

With a sigh, the dealer explains as gently as possible that if the stamp was in perfect condition it would be worth a penny or two, but in this condition it is worth precisely nothing, and might as well be consigned forthwith to the waste paper basket. The reaction may vary from shocked disappointment to downright disbelief.

The number of people whose hopes of a quick fortune have been shattered in this way is perhaps the unhappiest aspect of modern collecting. Thanks to the widespread publicity given to the sale of major rarities at auction, everyone is aware that stamps can be worth big money. The trouble is that non-collectors naturally enough assume that any stamp which is a century old must be of value from the fact of its age alone, and this, unfortunately, is far from the truth.

There are still quite a lot of stamps, first issued sixty, eighty or more years ago, which are still in plentiful supply and are likely to remain so for the foreseeable future. Of course it is not so easy to make this understood by a dear old lady who has a stamp which she feels sure must be a priceless antique just because it was left to her by Great Aunt Emma!

Some optimists even expect to receive a generous offer for stamps which the prospective purchaser has not even seen. I actually had a letter, some years ago, which went something like this: 'I have a red stamp from New Zealand. It looks very old. Please tell me how much I can get for it.'

Even if this correspondent had given full details of the stamp it would still have been impossible to give him a reliable answer. For one thing he could so easily have described the stamp wrongly from the catalogue – it is human nature to see a rare shade or variety in a stamp which is just the common one. For another thing, so much depends on the condition. So please don't expect a dealer or collector to give an opinion on stamps which he hasn't seen.

It is curious, too, how distrustful some people are of stamp dealers. They will cheerfully trust a jeweller to sell them a ring which contains real diamonds and not glass, but with stamps it's a different story!

I recall one man who told me he had a collection of Swiss stamps formed by his father around the turn of the century. He intended to offer the collection for sale to a dealer, but to make sure he would not be swindled, he would appreciate my independent opinion of its value!

I admit I was interested. Swiss stamps are very popular and a really good collection formed seventy years ago could be very valuable indeed today. When he produced the album, however, it didn't take long to see that such was not the case here. There were several quite nice stamps but many more damaged ones and nothing of much value. I told him that any offer of £5 or more for the whole collection would be fair, and he went off a sadder but wiser man.

Even the classic issues are not necessarily as valuable as some people suppose. The best example is perhaps the Penny Black itself. So many jump to the conclusion that because this is the oldest stamp it must also be worth the most money. On the face of it, the argument sounds fair enough. After all the unique character of the world's first stamp means that it is always in great demand. Moreover it was current for less than a year. Yet you can buy quite a presentable Penny Black for £5 or so, or less if you are content with an inferior example. I am referring, of course, to a used Penny Black. An unused one would be very much more expensive. So while it is naturally not a cheap stamp, it is certainly by no means one of the rarest.

Why should this be so? The answer lies in the habits of our early Victorian ancestors. Envelopes were rarely used in those days; letters were written on a sheet of paper which was then folded up and sealed, with the address and the stamp on the outside. Moreover the Victorians kept all their correspondence, often for very many years. At the same time a surprisingly large quantity of Penny Blacks were printed – more than sixty-eight millions of them altogether, and a considerable proportion of these have survived to find their way into collectors' albums, quite enough to prevent them from becoming great rarities. Indeed, the price would probably be less if there were not so many specialists who have acquired numbers of Penny Blacks to study the minor printing varieties on them. On the other hand it is quite unthinkable that the price of Penny Blacks should ever go down; on the contrary, a steady increase can be expected.

Stamp prices depend entirely on supply and demand. A stamp may be very rare but it will still not be worth very much if few collectors happen to want it. The stamp market, however, is international in character, and so is less likely to be greatly affected by economic conditions in any particular country. Because stamps are a world-wide hobby they have consistently shown their ability to retain and improve their value in the face of depreciating currencies.

Nowadays the better-class stamps, and especially the classics, are being increasingly bought by wealthy people as a hedge against inflation, and as they compete with one another for the choicer items, so the prices tend to go higher still.

But stamp prices can go down as well as up. This usually happens when a sudden craze develops for a particular

128

group or country. Prices are pushed up to unjustifiable levels in the rush, and then the reaction sets in.

In the years immediately after the Second World War, the stamps of King George VI were all the rage. But they lost some of their following on the change of sovereign, and the prices of the general run of such material tended to decline. Then in the 1950s, collectors rushed to buy Israel. Prices rocketed for a time, but then slipped back. This question of 'popular' and 'unpopular' countries is a curious aspect of the hobby, and anyone who can correctly predict which country's stamps are going to be in most demand in five years' time is on to a good thing!

When you start buying stamps, you may find several dealers offering the material you want to collect. Stamp dealing is a very individual sort of trade, and it will pay you to compare their prices carefully. But it is also worth bearing in mind that the dealer who keeps a good, general stock and provides an efficient, personal service may be more worthy of your support than one who is interested only in the gimmick of the moment.

Before long you may encounter the problem of the 'sleeper'. This is the term applied to a stamp whose scarcity is not generally recognised. It may be quoted at quite a low price in the catalogue, but no one seems to have it, and you have great trouble in locating one. Often such a stamp is an odd value from a definitive set for which there was not much postal demand at the time it was current, possibly because it covered a postage rate which became obsolete.

When tracking down a suspected 'sleeper', be prepared to pay something above the catalogue price. There is a lesson to be learned from the doubtless apocryphal story of pre-decimal days about the collector who went into a dealer's shop and asked the price of a particular stamp. The dealer produced it and said: 'It will cost you five shillings.'

'What!' exclaimed the collector. 'In so-and-so's shop down the road the price is only 3s. 6d.'

'In that case,' asked the dealer, 'why don't you buy it there?'

'Well it so happens that he doesn't have it in stock at the moment.'

'That explains it,' replied the dealer. 'When I haven't got that stamp in stock, my price is only half-a-crown!'

Some of these 'sleepers' can be identified by studying the columns of the philatelic tipsters in the stamp press. These writers tip certain stamps which they find to be in short supply for one reason or another and which are due, they believe, for a rise in price. Of course the fact that the stamps are thus publicly recommended is often enough in itself to push the price up! But the tips are usually sound enough and the collector who follows their advice and manages to obtain the stamps promptly will save himself money in the long run. Always provided, it should be added, that he satisfies himself with one or two copies only and doesn't become greedy. In time, however, the collector should find that with common sense and experience he will be able to work out his own ideas of the stamps most likely to increase in value.

If you are looking at stamps from the investment point of view, remember that it costs a dealer as much in time, effort and overheads to sell a stamp for a few pence as one for £5 or more. It follows, in general, that the cheaper the stamp, the greater the element of 'service' in the total price he must charge. If you are in the happy position of being able to spend £50 on stamps purely as an investment, you will do better to buy ten stamps at £5 each than 50 stamps at £1 each, and probably better still to buy five stamps at £10 each.

Remember, too, that common stamps are nearly always resold at a loss. But never mind! Think of the pleasure they will have given you before then. Whatever hobby you pursued you would expect it to cost you something. General collections consisting entirely of common stamps are usually a drug on the market: there are too many of them about and a dealer finds difficulty in disposing of them.

Successful investment in stamps, as in antique furniture or anything else, requires patience, study and knowledge. It should not be confused with mere speculation as practised, for example, by someone who tries to buy up large quantities of a particular stamp while it is still current in the hope that it will quickly go up in price as soon as it becomes obsolete. Plenty of people have burned their fingers that way in recent years.

So beware of tempting advertisements which promise spectacular profits from 'stamp investment', for it is usually speculation of this kind that they have in mind. Bearing in mind the supply-and-demand basis of stamp values, it is a matter of common sense that the mere fact that a stamp is held in large quantities means that it is unlikely to prove a good investment.

Of course there is one method of investing where you can hardly go wrong, provided you buy only from an entirely reputable source and you can spend enough money to make it worth while. I refer to the classics, the early issues of Great Britain and the British Colonies, Europe and the United States. These are the gilt-edged securities of philately which are marked up in the catalogues nearly every year. Here, condition is of paramount importance. It is a better proposition to pay a fair price for an item in really superb condition than a good deal less for something not quite so good.

Unfortunately this splendid material is beyond the means of most of us. For the average collector, and especially the beginner, it is far better to regard stamps as primarily a source of interest and recreation – with the chance of long-term financial appreciation as a pleasant but incidental bonus!

Above all, do not be misled into thinking that all you have

to do is to buy a few sheets of stamps from a popular country, put them by for a year or two, and then cash in. Just possibly you could be lucky – but more probably you won't. Obviously if a few other people have had the same idea the market will find difficulty in absorbing these supplies when the time comes for everyone to unload.

With rare exceptions dealers afford the only opportunity of disposing of stamps in quantity, and even if the stamps have increased in catalogue price a factor too often disregarded is the rather obvious one that the dealer's buying prices will be less than his selling prices. Like any other dealer he can only earn a living by making a profit. This means that the value of the stamps must go up by a third or more, i.e., the extent of the dealer's profit margin – before the speculator makes any profit at all. If the value goes up by less than that, he makes a loss.

Clearly the main pitfall of stamps as an investment lies in this question of disposal when the investor decides to sell out. The ideal way, of course, is to find another collector interested in what you have to sell, and come to terms with him. But that is more easily said than done.

Circulating exchange packets are a splendid means of disposing of oddments and duplicates, but hardly of whole collections or single stamps in quantity. In any case there is the rather laborious task of mounting and pricing the stamps for sale. You are likely to wait some months for your money, and at the end of it all some of the stamps are likely to remain unsold.

You will stand a better chance of getting a good price from a dealer if the material is neatly arranged to indicate exactly what is there. This not only avoids the risk of the dealer overlooking some particular feature but also makes it easier for him to re-sell if he is contemplating 'breaking up' the collection into sections before offering it to his customers. In large accumulations particularly it is advisable to keep the mint stamps separate from the used, because that is the way the dealer will re-sell them. In the case of more advanced material, it is a good idea to offer it to a dealer who specializes in the stamps concerned. He will have many specialist collectors on his books and with a more likely market he will be able to offer a better price.

Another method of disposing of stamps is at auction. The big advantage here is the truly international publicity arranged for their sales by the leading auctioneers. The vendor who entrusts his material to one of these firms knows that his stamps will be brought to the notice of virtually all the main buyers in the whole world. The auctioneers employ experienced philatelists to describe the lots on offer, and such is the confidence felt by the stamp world in these descriptions that a large proportion of the bidding is postal.

On the other hand there will be the auctioneer's commission to pay; and many of the bidders at the big auctions are leading dealers, who will not pay more than their usual buying price if they can help it!

Some people will tell you that the financial side looms too large in the present state of the hobby; that too many collectors are interested only in the value of their stamps. There may be some truth in this, and it is certainly a mistake for beginners to place too much emphasis on the investment approach. But provided that it is not taken to excess I still consider that the financial aspect of stamp collecting gives the hobby a certain piquancy which it would otherwise lack.

Whatever the disadvantages of stamps as an investment – and there are many – it remains true that provided a collector buys wisely over the years he will probably, when the time comes to dispose of his collection, get most if not all of his money back, and perhaps a profit into the bargain. Of how many hobbies can that be said? After all, you don't expect to sell a set of golf clubs for as much as you gave for them after they have given you many years of enjoyment!

For those fascinated by the thought of huge sums of

money, it may be worth mentioning as footnote to this chapter that stamps enable you to become a multi-millionaire, at least on paper, at the minimum of cost. You can do this by collecting stamps of the wilder inflationary periods.

Germany set the pattern when, at the height of inflation in 1923, a stamp with a face value of 1,000 million marks was issued. But even this figure was far exceeded at the end of the Second World War and nowhere did stamp denominations rise to such astronomical levels as in Hungary.

During the war years it was never necessary to issue a stamp of more than 5 pengos face value. But within a few months of the war ending a stamp of 3,000 pengos was required. That was just the beginning of the collapse. Stamps were issued first in thousands of pengos, then in millions, then in thousands of millions, and finally in millions of millions. Large quantities of stamps were produced in identical designs and colours, leaving the values to be printed in at the last moment in an effort to keep pace with postal rates which rose almost daily. Eventually the highest value reached was 500,000 million million pengos.

By this time there was insufficient space on the stamp to accommodate the required row of noughts, so instead there was a numeral followed by 'BILLIO P.', standing for millions of millions of pengos.

And these curious stamps are still catalogued at only a few pence each! For anyone hoping that stamps will make him a millionaire, this is the easiest way of achieving it – on paper, at any rate.

If you look upon stamps just as a way of making money, you will almost certainly be disappointed. But if you look upon a collection as a fascinating pastime which with luck and good judgment may eventually appreciate in value, you can look forward to many years of increasing pleasure and interest.

CHAPTER SIXTEEN

THE WAY AHEAD

The word *philatelie* was devised as long ago as 1864 by a Frenchman who coined it from two Greek words – *Philos* (friend) and *a-telia* (free from charge or tax). Thus one who liked things that gave exemption from charges, i.e. stamps, was a philatelist. Curiously enough the French nowadays prefer the term *timbrologie* to describe the hobby, but in English philately is firmly established. As regards pronunciation, the emphasis in the noun is on the second syllable, phiLATely, but in the adjective it is on the third, philaTELic.

So far in this book the terms philately and stamp collecting have been used as virtually interchangeable, but many people would say that this is not correct. Whereas the great majority of philatelists are stamp collectors (unless they are solely postal historians!) not all stamp collectors can be regarded as philatelists.

A collector may just amass stamps in a higgledy-piggledy manner without plan or order, but a philatelist is one who methodically studies the stamps which he collects. A relative newcomer to the hobby can therefore soon aspire to the title of philatelist: to my way of thinking it is not a description to be reserved only for advanced specialists!

To become a philatelist thus resolves itself into learning more about stamps, and there are many ways of doing this: from your fellow collectors, from stamp exhibitions, from meetings of your local philatelic society, and from the philatelic press.

Britain is fortunate in the high standard of its philatelic press and there is a wide range of journals to choose from. It is a good idea for the beginner to give all the principal ones a fair trial and find out which ones suit him best.

There are two weeklies: the old-established *Stamp Collecting*, founded before the First World War, which is an excellent magazine for the average collector; and the more recent *Stamp Weekly*, started in 1967, which is in tabloid newspaper format and places more emphasis on the stamp market.

Among the monthlies may be noted the *Philatelic Magazine* (which was a fortnightly until 1970), *Stamp Magazine* and *Stamp Monthly*. The last named is the house magazine of Stanley Gibbons Ltd. and until 1970 it was known as *Gibbons' Stamp Monthly*. It is valuable for its monthly supplements and lists of price alterations to the Gibbons catalogues. In addition there are a number of journals, generally of a more specialized or advanced character, published by various firms and societies.

The advertising pages of these periodicals are frequently of just as much interest as the pages of philatelic news and the articles. The house journals, of course, can be expected to carry only the advertisements of their publishers, but the others contain numerous offers of stamps old and new, sets, collections, approvals and the rest. The advertisements give readers a useful guide to the progress of stamp values, and are particularly helpful to collectors who do not live within easy reach of a dealer. In any case the vast majority of stamps are bought and sold through the post, and this applies even to dealers who have successful shops in the big towns.

Among the many valuable services which the philatelic press renders to the hobby, not the least are the reviews of new literature to be found in its pages. For some reason collectors as a breed seem to be notoriously mean when it comes to supporting philatelic literature. Over a year they may spend quite a considerable sum on stamps, yet they seem strangely reluctant to venture a pound or two on a new book by an expert which may vastly increase their knowledge and pleasure and may well repay its cost many times over, perhaps by enabling them to identify a hitherto unsuspected scarce stamp in their collections!

Too often in the past sales of many a specialized book have proved disappointing, bringing poor reward to the writer and publisher for their trouble. Then when the book is at last out of print, everyone is after it and second-hand copies start to fetch high prices.

Good philatelic literature is thus a wise investment from every point of view. Before taking up any new philatelic interest, always find out what literature is available and thereafter watch out for any new publications on the subject which may be noticed by the stamp periodicals.

Advanced literature may vary in size and style from small booklets in paper covers to weighty volumes. They are often known as handbooks or monographs. They deal in detail with the philatelic story of one particular country or area; or they may be highly specialized studies of one particular issue or even, in extreme cases, one particular stamp! One thing they have in common: all are written by experienced specialists who record their knowledge as a labour of love for the benefit of fellow enthusiasts. The printing of such books is necessarily small in number and the retail price correspondingly high when compared with other kinds of books; nevertheless, for collectors interested in the subject, they are indeed money well spent.

To join the ranks of true philatelists requires some knowledge of the manufacture of stamps, and this begins with the actual design. A stamp design before it is accepted, or an unaccepted design, is known as an essay. Proofs are simply trial prints of a stamp. A proof taken from the engraver's original die is called a die proof; if taken from the printing plate, it is a plate proof.

The printing processes most likely to be encountered in stamps are four in number. In a recess-printed stamp, the printed part of the design is recessed into the printing plate. Ink is applied to the surface which is then carefully wiped, forcing the ink into the crevices. When the paper is passed through the press under pressure, it takes up the ink from the recesses in the plate. Naturally the shallower recesses carry less ink than the deeper ones, and in this way the printer obtains varying intensities of colour. The majority of the very early stamps, known as the line-engraved issues, were produced by this method.

In a typographed or surface-printed stamp the principle is reversed. The printed part of the design stands up in relief on the printing plate, and the ink is transferred from this to the paper. This process is also known as letterpress.

A third process, quite different from the others, is lithography, which involves printing from a flat surface. Lithography depends on the fact that grease and water will not mix. The design is applied to the printing surface by a greasy agent, the non-printing parts being treated with water. In this way only those parts which are to be printed attract the ink, while the other parts repel it. In the modern development of offset-lithography, the design is transferred to a rubber roller which in turn transmits it to the paper.

Photogravure, used for many attractive modern multi-coloured stamps, is really a kind of recess printing. But in this case the design is reproduced photographically on the printing surface, a screen breaking up the detail into thousands of tiny squares which are etched to varying depths. By this means graduations of colour are produced, the fineness of the design varying according to the coarseness or otherwise of the screen.

An ancillary process, very little used for stamps nowadays owing to its high cost, is embossing. This involves raising parts of the actual stamp in relief, either coloured or uncoloured. The British 6d., 1od. and 1s. stamps of 1847–54 had the head of Queen Victoria embossed, as did certain stamps of Heligoland and the early issues of the Gambia-the very attractive stamps known to collectors as the Cameos.

How do you distinguish stamps produced by the different processes? With a little practice it is not at all difficult.

In a recess-printed stamp the ink stands up in ridges on the paper. This is clearly seen with the aid of a magnifier, but can usually be detected simply by passing the finger-tip lightly over the surface, when the ridges will be apparent to the touch. Photogravure stamps are readily identified by their photograph-like appearance, and the magnifier quickly picks out the distinctive squares of graded colour.

Typographed stamps have a typical 'bite'; by examining the back of the stamp the design can be seen impressed into the paper. Lithographed stamps, in contrast, have a flat, smooth appearance, lacking the characteristics of the other processes.

Substantial books have been published which describe the manufacture of stamps in detail, and these may be studied later on with profit and pleasure. But for a start this basic ability to distinguish the most important printing processes is helpful in various ways. For one thing it will enable you to spot very quickly some of the more obvious forgeries, which were often produced by the wrong process. It will also aid your understanding when you come to undertake more specialized collecting.

A stamp that remains in use for a number of years goes through numerous printings, and no matter how careful the printers may be in matching up a new printing with the previous one, it is inevitable that minor variations will creep in over a period of time. Again, while a printing plate is actually in use it may develop flaws which show up on the stamps. If the flaws become really noticeable they may well be repaired – resulting in further varieties, known as retouches, for the philatelist.

At the same time a slightly different ink may be introduced, resulting in an identifiable shade, or for some reason the watermark may be changed or the stamps may be perforated to a different gauge.

Thus the specialist gradually builds up in his collection a complete history of a particular issue or stamp. With the help of blocks and strips of stamps, especially any that have part of the sheet margin attached, it may be possible to learn the position in the sheet from which each flaw comes. In some cases the expert, by close examination, can even identify the correct position of every single stamp in the sheet! When by dint of much patient search he has assembled the whole lot in the right sequence, he is said to have a reconstructed sheet.

Obviously such detailed study is not everyone's cup of tea, and countless people have enjoyed collecting stamps without ever specializing to this extent. But many collectors are drawn to this form of advance philately sooner or later. It has two advantages: such a collection has no real end, making it a lifetime's interest for those who like it, and it can be carried out with inexpensive stamps which are easily obtainable for study in quantity. Specialization certainly calls for more time and effort than straightforward collecting, but not necessarily a great deal of expense.

As a rule only constant varieties are considered to be worth collecting, that is to say, varieties which appear consistently in the same position on each sheet throughout a particular printing, or at least part of it. Perhaps a speck of dust may land on the printing plate, causing a blob of ink to appear on the stamp, but it may well disappear after only one or two sheets have been printed. This ephemeral kind of variety, unless it is of a really spectacular nature, is of much less interest to a specialist than one which is constant.

Again, the only varieties worthy of a specialist's attention are those properly issued by the post office. Cases have been known where varieties of a most startling kind have appeared on the market, varieties which have subsequently proved to be printer's waste which should have been destroyed but which has surreptitiously emerged through the back door of the printing works!

On recess-printed stamps one of the most popular kinds of variety is the re-entry. When a worn impression on the printing plate is erased and replaced by another, it happens that sometimes a few traces of the old one remain, appearing as a duplication of certain parts of the design. Frequently this is only clearly apparent with the aid of a magnifier. Re-entries are especially keenly sought after in the early line-engraved stamps of Great Britain, but can also be found from time to time on quite modern issues. In the latter cases the ideal way of collecting re-entries is in positional blocks, i.e. blocks of stamps extending to the nearest sheet margin to indicate the position of the varieties.

Some of the best-known re-entries and certain other major varieties are listed in the general catalogues and are quoted at high prices. To attain such recognition, however, they must usually be clearly visible with the unaided eye, and if you are thinking of buying varieties as an investment, this is a good principle to follow. Otherwise the best way of acquiring varieties is by using your knowledge and observation to get them at the same price as the normal stamp! Nevertheless, a well arranged specialized collection of a popular country will certainly be worth more than the individual stamps contained in it.

A word of caution is due about shades. A stamp listed in the general catalogue with two or three shades may have a dozen in a specialized publication. But colours exist only in the eye of the beholder, so beware of paying good money for what is claimed to be a rare shade, simply because the other fellow thinks it is one! If, on the other hand, you can obtain what you consider to be strikingly different shades of a stamp, all at the normal price, that's fair enough. Bear in mind, too, that climatic conditions can affect stamp colours. Put one or two common stamps in your window, leave them there in the summer sunshine for a week or two, and you will probably find that you have 'manufactured' a new shade or two for yourself! Some stamps have had their colour changed completely through climatic or chemical action, and these are known in the hobby as colour changelings.

Quite apart from variations which arise in the actual printing, another group are caused by differences in the paper. Some issues can be found on both thick and thin paper; there are some scarce thin-paper varieties among modern Australian stamps. You may also come across occasionally a very thin, brittle paper called pelure. Thickness apart, two main types of paper are involved in philately: laid and wove. In laid paper, the fibres appear to run across the stamp, either vertically or horizontally. The great majority of stamps, however, are printed on ordinary wove paper, in which this feature is absent.

With watermarks, too, there are two main kinds. A watermark so placed as to come neatly in the centre of each stamp is a single watermark. This was the sort used in the early days. In the case of a multiple watermark, the device is repeated at close intervals all over the sheet, so that several whole ones and parts of several others may appear on a single stamp. Rarely you may also encounter an example of a sheet watermark: one large device, frequently a coat-of-arms, spread over the sheet, so that any one stamp will show at best only a small part of it, and perhaps none at all. A growing proportion of the world's stamps, it should be added, are now printed without watermark of any kind.

The method of measuring perforations has already been described, but in addition to differences of gauge there are two principal kinds of perforation, comb and line. Line perforation is where the perforating machine punches one line of perforations at a time; comb perforation, which is much more common and nowadays practically universal, is so called because in this case the perforating pins are arranged somewhat like a comb perforating three sides of the stamp, row by row, at one operation. Irregularity of perforation holes where stamps meet is an indication of line perforation; it is best seen, of course, in blocks of four stamps or more.

Another type of separation has been used occasionally on stamps; this is called rouletting, and it consists of a series of slits cut into the paper between the stamps. The great difference between rouletting and perforation is that in the former case no paper is actually removed, whereas the perforating machine does in fact punch out tiny circles of paper.

Errors of perforation provide many varieties for the specialist: stamps partly perforated, or perforated in the wrong place, or a pair of stamps without perforations between them. The so-called 'interrupted perfs' of the Netherlands, issued between 1926 and 1939, were quite deliberate, being applied to stamps intended for use in vending machines. Some modern Australian stamps issued for a similar purpose have both large and small perforation holes.

Even in specialized collecting you will gain more satisfaction from the hobby if you remember to keep in mind the geographic and historical background of the stamps. You may find that during the Second World War the stamps of a remote British colony suddenly appeared with a new perforation – the result of a printing works in Britain being put out of action in the blitz. By specializing in nineteenth century France you can see the effects of the Franco-Prussian war, when the printing of stamps was hurriedly transferred to Bordeaux. In 1923 Japanese stamps were issued without gum in the difficult conditions following the disastrous earthquake of that year. And so one could go on.

By collecting stamps you can open a new window on the world without moving from your fireside. By taking the way ahead from the mere accumulation of stamps to the interests of real philately you can open the window wider still.

143

APPENDIX

SOME PHILATELIC
TERMS EXPLAINED

Like every other pursuit, stamp collecting has its own ter-
minology – its jargon, if you like – which includes a few
expressions which mean something rather different in
philately than they do in ordinary, everyday English! Here
then is a short alphabetical glossary of the terms which the
beginner is most likely to encounter, and whose meaning
may not be immediately obvious.

Agency   A postal agency operated by a post office outside its
   own national territory, for example the British postal
   agencies in the Persian Gulf area; or an organisation
   promoting sales of new issues to the stamp trade on behalf
   of the issuing governments.
Aerogramme   International term for an airletter sheet, light-
   weight postal stationery intended for airmail at a lower
   rate of postage.
Albino   An impression of a stamp which has accidentally
   escaped inking. Or uncoloured embossing.
Aniline   A type of fugitive ink, used in the printing of certain stamps, which shows flourescence under ultra-violet
   rays.
'As is'   Term used mostly by auctioneers to indicate that an
   item is offered 'as it is', i.e. without any kind of guarantee.
Backstamp   Postmark applied to the back of a postal item,
   frequently indicating the date of arrival.
Backprint   Any printing on the reverse side of a stamp.
Bantams   Stamps of small size (showing a most unusual
   mixture of perforation and rouletting) issued by South

Africa as a paper-saving measure during the Second World War.

Bilingual pair   Two stamps joined together, one inscribed in one language, the other in another. For example South African stamps alternately inscribed in English and Afrikaans.

Bisect   A stamp cut into two halves, each part designed to pay postage to the extent of half the face value of the complete stamp.

Block   Four or more unseparated stamps from adjoining rows. (Three or more unseparated stamps from the same row are known as a strip.)

Booklet pane   A complete 'page' of stamps from a stamp booklet.

Burelage   A fine pattern of faint lines or dots printed underneath the main design, or on the back of the stamp. For example, the early stamps of Denmark.

Cachet   Any marking, design or inscription on a cover which describes the special circumstances in which it was posted.

Cancelled to order   Term applied to stamps cancelled by the post office without the stamps having gone through the post. Frequently abbreviated to 'c.t.o.'

Centred   A stamp correctly placed between the perforations leaving an equal margin all round, is said to be 'well-centred', and is usually preferred to one which is 'off centre'.

Chalky paper   A chalk-coated, highly surfaced paper sometimes used for stamp printing. Such stamps require especially careful handling to avoid damaging the surface.

Charity stamps   Issues sold at a higher price than the postal value, the surcharge being applied to some charitable organisation.

Check letters   Letters found in the corners of early stamps of Great Britain, indicating the position on the sheet.

Coils   Stamps printed in large rolls or coils, instead of sheets, often for use in vending machines.

Colour trials   Proofs of a stamp design in various colours, from which the selection is made as to the colour in which the issued stamp is to be printed.

Column   Complete vertical row of stamps.

Combination cover   A cover bearing the stamps of two different stamp-issuing authorities.

Control   Control letters and/or numbers printed on the sheet margins of British stamps between 1881 and 1947 as an accounting aid. The term is also applied to any security measure (overprinting, etc.) applied to a stamp to deter pilferage.

Cover   Complete envelope, wrapper or outer letter-sheet as transmitted by post.

Cuts-outs   Non-adhesive stamps cut out from items of postal stationery.

Demonetised   No longer valid for postage.

Die   The piece of metal on which the original design is engraved and which is subsequently multiplied to produce the plate from which stamps are printed.

'Dues'   Familiar name for Postage Due stamps.

Duty plate   Printing plate used for adding the inscriptions (name of country, face value, etc.) to stamps of which the main design is printed from a key plate.

Entire   A complete folded letter-sheet with the message on the inside and the address on the outside. The meaning of the term is sometimes extended to include covers of other kinds.

'Face'   Abbreviation for face value. Thus a used 20p stamp offered at 'half face' will cost 10p.

Forerunner   Historical predecessor of a country, group or issue. Thus the stamps of Palestine are the forerunners of those of Israel, and British stamps used in the West Indies may be regarded as forefunners of those islands' own stamps.

Frank A signature or postal marking indicating that the letter is to be carried post free.

Graphite Line Name given to the British stamps issued in 1957 with vertical lines of graphite on the backs – introduced in connection with the experimental installation of an electronic letter-facing machine. They were subsequently replaced with stamps showing phosphor lines on the front.

Gutter Unprinted space between stamps, or between panes of stamps making up a complete sheet.

Handstamp A postmark (not an adhesive stamp) applied by hand.

Imprint The printer's name inscribed on the sheet margin, or (occasionally) beneath each stamp. An imprint block is a block of four or more stamps with sheet margin attached showing the printer's name.

Interprovincial A stamp issued by one province of South Africa but used in another, subsequent to the formation of the Union of South Africa.

Invalidated No longer valid for postage.

Jubilee Line Thick coloured line on the margin around a sheet or pane of stamps, designed to prevent excessive wear on the edges of the plate, and so called because it was introduced in British stamp printing in 1887, the year of Queen Victoria's jubilee.

Key plate The plate used for printing that part of a stamp design common to more than one value or country, the distinctive details being added by means of a duty plate. The system was widely used in the past by Great Britain, France, Portugal and Spain for the stamps of their respective colonies.

Label Any adhesive item not valid for postage; also applied, as a term of disparagement, to bogus stamps.

Maltese Cross The cancellation used on the early stamps of Great Britain, between 1840 and 1844. The Maltese

Crosses used in many different towns can be identified and are keenly studied by specialists.

Maximum card   A picture postcard featuring a similar subject to the stamp with which the card is franked.

Multiple   Any group of unseparated stamps more than two in number.

Obsolete   No longer available over the post office counter. When remaining stocks of a stamp are being used up while its successor is also on sale, it is said to be obsolescent.

Omnibus Issue   Group of stamps, frequently sharing a common design, issued by a number of countries to commemorate the same occasion; e.g. the Silver Jubilee series of 1935.

On paper   With part of the cover still adhering to the stamp. Stamps which have been removed from the cover are said to be 'off paper'.

On piece   With sufficient of the original cover still adhering to the stamp to show the complete cancellation or other postal markings.

Pane   A sub-division of a complete sheet, usually a half or quarter, separate from the rest by gutters.

Perfin   A stamp with a device or initials perforated into it. Otherwise known as a 'Spif' (Stamp perforated with initials of firm).

Phosphor Line   Lines of phosphor applied to the stamps of Great Britain since 1959 for use in connection with electronic letter-facing machines – replacing the earlier Graphite Line. Subsequently adopted by several other countries, the phosphor lines can be easily seen on mint stamps by holding them horizontally to a strong light.

Pre-stamp cover   Cover postally used prior to the introduction of adhesive postage stamps in the country of origin. Also referred to as a pre-adhesive cover.

Quartz lamp   An electric lamp emitting ultra-violet rays, a valuable aid in the detection of forgeries and fakes.

Regionals   Certain stamps of Great Britain produced in

special versions for Scotland, Wales, Northern Ireland and the Isle of Man; also formerly for Jersey and Guernsey.

Remainder   Stock of stamps remaining in post office hands after the issue has been officially withdrawn from sale. They are normally destroyed, but a few cases have occurred of remainders being disposed of at cut prices.

Reprints   Stamps of an obsolete issue reprinted from the original plate. Not to be confused with new printings, which refer to stamps still current.

Se-tenant   Joined together; i.e. unseparated.

Short set   A set of stamps complete up to a specified value only, excluding the more expensive higher values.

Souvenir sheet   A miniature sheet of stamps produced more as a souvenir than for postal purposes, usually incorporating some commemorative inscription or design on the sheet margin. The term may also include certain items of philatelic interest but no postal validity, such as the sheets formerly produced in connection with STAMPEX.

'Space filler'   A stamp not of first-class condition but good enough to fill a space in a collection for the time being.

Specimen   Stamps overprinted or perforated with the word 'Specimen' or its equivalents are samples forwarded for reference purposes to the Universal Postal Union.

Strip   Three or more unseparated stamps in a horizontal or vertical row.

Tab   Perforated section of sheet margin bearing appropriate inscription or design, a regular feature of Israeli issues.

Tête-bêche   Head to tail; i.e. a pair of unseparated stamps in which one is upside down in relation to the other.

Thinned   A stamp of which the surface may be intact but the paper has lost some of its original thickness when seen from the back is said to be thinned. Such damage has a severely adverse effect on the value of a rare stamp.

Tied   A stamp on cover or piece, with a cancellation

extending from the stamp on to the cover, is said to be 'tied'.

Underprint   A design or pattern underlying the main design of the stamp. Printing on the back of a stamp is sometimes referred to as an underprint, but is better described as a backprint.

Value panel   That part of a stamp design which indicates the face value.

Vignette   The central part of a pictorial stamp as opposed to the frame or border.

War stamps, War tax   Stamps issued with a surcharge to raise funds in time of war.

Wing margin   Prior to 1880, certain British stamps were printed in sheets in which the gutters were perforated down the centre, resulting in the central marginal stamps having one wide and exaggerated margin. These 'wing-margined' stamps were formerly unpopular with collectors because of their unbalanced shape, but are in fact, of course, scarcer than the normal stamps.

Zemstvos   Local stamps issued by local authorities in Czarist Russia.

Many other philatelic terms are explained in the main text of this book.

The beginner may also find it helpful to study the following list of abbreviations which are widely used in the hobby.

A.P.O.   Army Post Office.

B.W.I.   British West Indies.

C.   In catalogues, chalky paper. In tables of relative value, common.

C.A.   Crown Agents.

C.C.   Crown Colonies.

C.T.O.   Cancelled to order.

Cat.   Catalogue, or catalogue value.

Des.   Design, or designed by.

F.D.C.   First-day cover.

F.P.O.   Field Post Office.

F.U.   Fine used.

G.B.   Great Britain.

Imperf.   Imperforate – without perforations or rouletting.

Invtd.   Inverted (upside down).

K.E.VII   King Edward VII.

K.G.V   King George V.

K.G.VI   King George VI.

Litho.   Lithographed.

M.   Mint.

Min. sht.   Miniature sheet.

Mult.   Multiple.

O.   Ordinary paper (not chalky).

O.g.   Original gum.

Opt.   Overprint.

Perf.   Perforation or perforated.

Phos.   Phosphor-lined or phosphor treated.

Photo.   Photogravure.

Pl.   Plate.

Pmk.   Postmark.

Q.V.   Queen Victoria.

Q.E.II   Queen Elizabeth II.

R, RR, RRR   Used in some auction catalogues to denote degrees of rarity.

R.D.P.   Roll of Distinguished Philatelists.

S.G.   Stanley Gibbons.

T.P.O.   Travelling Post Office.

T.R.D.   Temporary rubber datestamp.

Typo.   Typographed.

U.   Used.

Un.   Unused.

Uncat.   Uncatalogued.

Var.   Variety.

Wmk.   Watermark.

INDEX

Beginner's Guide to
Tropical Fish and Fish Tanks

REGINALD DUTTA

Techniques improve very rapidly in this thriving, fast
changing industry—aerators, filters, tanks, heating and
lighting are clear examples, and you need to be guided by a
man who really knows the field. This book is produced from
within the very heart of the industry; the author is the
Managing Director of London's oldest-established tropical
fish specialists.

The book is written from the customer's point of view.
It's information and guidance will save many a needless
headache and useless expense, and make your tank pleasant
and pleasing.

Sphere   40p

Beginner's Guide to Coarse Fishing

ARTHUR E. HARDY

Whether you take up coarse fishing for sport, relaxation or pure pleasure, a good 'starter' book can go a long way to eliminating some of the guesswork, explain the mysteries of modern fishing tackle and spell out, in simple detail, the wide variety of baits, methods and other 'wrinkles' that could mean the difference between a blank day and a worthwhile catch.

This is such a book. The easy to follow text takes the novice step by step into the watery world of each species of coarse fish – how, when and where it feeds and the right tackle, baits and methods for its successful and most sporting capture.

Sphere   40p

Beginner's Guide to Bridge

NORMAN SQUIRE

Norman Squire first played bridge for England in 1946 and
for sixteen years was Competition Editor for 'Bridge
Magazine' where his problems and articles 'contributed
more original and valuable thought to the game than has
anyone else since the war', and his teaching there and in
periodicals and newspapers throughout the world did much
to modernize the methods of even the best players. His
tournament record has been called outstanding and includes
repeated wins of the major British Championships.

In this book he provides a clear and comprehensive guide
that is aimed directly at reducing the labour of learning in a
fashion that will appeal to anyone seeking to master the art
of bridge.

Sphere   40p

All Sphere Books are available at your bookshop or
newsagent, or can be ordered from the following address:

Sphere Books, Cash Sales Department,
P.O. Box 11, Falmouth, Cornwall.

Please send cheque or postal order (no currency), and allow
7p per book to cover the cost of postage and packing
in U.K., 7p per copy overseas.